American Girl®

Cross-Stitch

EASY-TO-FOLLOW PATTERNS INSPIRED BY THE DOLLS WE LOVE

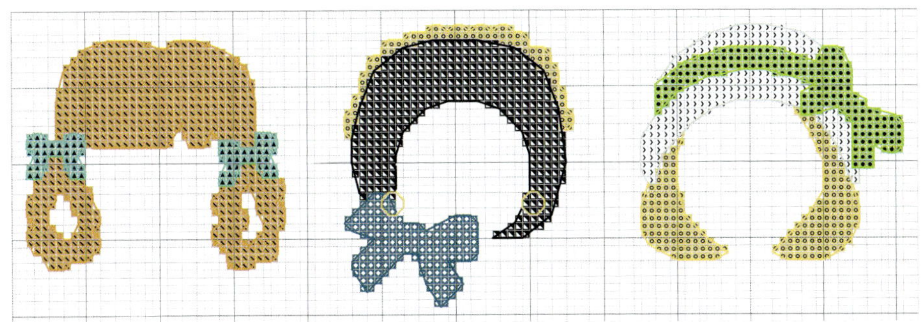

SOSAE CAETANO AND
DENNIS CAETANO

RUNNING PRESS
PHILADELPHIA

Running Press
Hachette Book Group
1290 Avenue of the Americas, New York, NY 10104
www.runningpress.com
@Running_Press

First Edition: April 2026

Published by Running Press, an imprint of Hachette Book Group, Inc. The Running Press name and logo are trademarks of Hachette Book Group, Inc.

The Hachette Speakers Bureau provides a wide range of authors for speaking events. To find out more, go to www.hachettespeakersbureau.com or email HachetteSpeakers@hbgusa.com.

Running Press books may be purchased in bulk for business, educational, or promotional use. For more information, please contact your local bookseller or the Hachette Book Group Special Markets Department at Special.Markets@hbgusa.com.

The publisher is not responsible for websites (or their content) that are not owned by the publisher.

Print book cover and interior design by Frances J. Soo Ping Chow
Patterns stitched by Rachel Bender

Library of Congress Cataloging-in-Publication Data has been applied for.

ISBNs: 978-0-7624-8875-9 (paperback),
978-0-7624-8877-3 (ebook)

Printed in China

APS

10 9 8 7 6 5 4 3 2

Contents

Introduction

When Pleasant Rowland founded American Girl (then Pleasant Company) in 1986, her dream was to inspire and educate young girls through play. Molly McIntire, Samantha Parkington, and Kirsten Larson were the original trio of Historical Characters—embodying characters out of storybooks and telling history from their perspective. Their unique personalities, (mis)adventures, and life lessons inspired a generation of girls, showing what was possible in a world where they're often dismissed and underestimated. In a word, the characters and their stories were and continue to be empowering.

Since then, American Girl has expanded and diversified the array of dolls, books, and accessories available. First-generation American Girl fans (OGs) continue to gravitate to the brand, fueling a kind of nostalgia revolution. With a unique blend of social, political, and cultural awareness, modern-day fans have taken what they learned from the original characters and stories and made them relevant to the here and now.

Beautiful dolls, and play in general, are not just for kids anymore. Adult American Girl fans know enough to take their fun seriously. Older fans often enjoy meetups at the American Girl Café, author signings, and store shopping events. Best of all, as grown-up fans, shopping means not having to ask for what you want (which usually involves a doll-haul, with clothes and accessories, of course!).

If you're an OG American Girl fan, welcome to an all-new crafty adventure with your favorite Historical Characters. If you're new to the world of American Girl and have crafty inclinations, you've found a place where you belong. Because if there's any one theme that runs through the stories of these bold and brave girls, it's finding that place of belonging. Now you can do it one stitch at a time.

What Is Cross-Stitch?

Cross-stitch is an age-old craft. Old as time, as they say. American Girl fans understand the depth and meaning of those words. (Especially those lucky kids who got the original Pleasant Company craft books associated with each Historical Character!)

If you don't know the details already, cross-stitch is a kind of embroidery done on gridded fabric such as Aida or evenweave. It's a meditative and detail-oriented art. It's as fun as long summer days and as cozy as cool autumn afternoons. If you have even an inkling of interest in needlecraft, or the smallest bit of cross-stitch curiosity, then

you're in for a treat—not to mention a lifelong passion. Cross-stitchers are like American Girl fans: dedicated, devoted, and touched with revolutionary spirit, with a soft spot for all things quaint.

AMERICAN GIRL AND CROSS-STITCH

American Girl and cross-stitch are just about the most natural pair one can imagine—quaint and charming. Both have endured throughout American history, recording past events and personal stories. Cross-stitch is, fundamentally, a storytelling craft.

The patterns in this book are a celebration of the enduring spirit of the American Girl brand. They're also a wink and a nod to nostalgia, which runs deep in the heart of adult AG fandom.

Start by stitching the iconic AG logo and star. Devotees of Molly, Samantha, Addy, and the rest of the Historical Characters will love connecting with their favorite doll through the "I'm a(n) . . ." patterns. Those who grew up learning about themselves while thumbing the pages of *The Care & Keeping of You* will love the perfectly frameable project by the same name. "Meet Me at the Café" and "Raised by American Girl" are modern-day memes-turned-identifiers, connecting fans across time and space. There are patterns for every skill level and devotion, including hair silhouettes, clothing and accessories, decorative signs, and sweet tributes to the timeless cuteness of American Girl.

Each pattern in this book features the following information to help make your project a success:

DIFFICULTY: The difficulty of each pattern ranges from easy to intermediate to advanced. Difficulty levels are determined by the amount and intricacy of backstitches as well as the number of cross-stitch color changes. Size is not necessarily a part of the equation, as you'll notice a number of large patterns are labeled "easy," while a few of the much smaller ones are labeled "advanced." If you're new to cross-stitch, choose an easy pattern for your first project. This will help ensure success and build affinity for this wonderful craft. It's always fun to jump right into a challenge, but we encourage every newbie to have at least one easy project under their belt before embarking on intermediate and advanced designs.

THREAD COLORS: This is the list of DMC-brand floss colors you'll need to stitch each project. (You can use other non-DMC-brand floss but be sure to try and match the colors to the DMC colors as closely as possible.)

FINISHED SIZE: This is the approximate size of each finished cross-stitch. Given in inches, this information is helpful to know and is especially useful when planning a project with your finished cross-stitch. For example, if you're trying to find just the right design for making a greeting card or wall-hanging banner (see "Fun American Girl Cross-Stitch Projects" on how to make these), you'll need to know the finished size of the design.

APPROXIMATE STITCH TIME: This lets you know about how long it will take to finish a project in one sitting. Of course, cross-stitch projects are normally done in parts over many days, weeks, and sometimes months. Don't be daunted by approximate stitch times. Use them as a guide to determine how much time you will likely spend with a given project. Keep in mind it's always nice to have an ongoing cross-stitch project as a means of regular relaxation and creativity. If you think of stitch times that way, you can even have multiple projects going at once—a short-term instant-gratification project and a longer-term passion project.

AIDA FABRIC SIZE: This is the recommended size to cut your Aida fabric for each project. You can make it bigger but not smaller. This size accommodates the cross-stitch itself and includes an additional 2-inch border. The extra space around the project is necessary for all finishing techniques, like turning your cross-stitch into a banner or hoop art. More on that in the chapter "Fun Projects."

DISPLAY HOOP SIZE: Because most stitchers love the simplicity and ease of using a cross-stitch hoop to display their finished masterpiece, we've included a recommended hoop size.

Throughout this book you'll also find a lot of helpful tips. Take them to heart for a more enjoyable stitching experience.

And because American Girl is all about friendship, fun, and learning, throughout the book you'll find facts, anecdotes, and quirky tidbits about your favorite characters. If you're a lifelong fan, these details will be a cool throwback. If you're a new fan, you'll get to learn more about the wonderful world of American Girl.

It's All in the Basics

TOOLS AND TECHNIQUES

To stitch the beautiful American Girl patterns in this book, you'll need a few basic tools. Fortunately, cross-stitch is a very welcoming craft, with easy-to-find supplies. A quick trip to your local craft store, or any online needlework or craft shop, and you'll find everything listed below.

Cross-Stitch Fabric

AIDA: Aida is a sturdy gridded fabric designed specifically for cross-stitching. It comes in various grid sizes, such as 10-count, 14-count, and 18-count. (The grid gets smaller as the number gets larger.) Note that designs stitched on 10-count Aida will be much larger than if they were stitched on 18-count Aida. Keep this in mind when planning your stitchwork. Aida is ideal for novice stitchers and a favorite of seasoned stitchers who appreciate its versatility and ease of use. Fourteen-count white Aida is the most popular variety, and it's readily available at craft stores and online. Aida comes in countless colors, light and dark, which allows for lots of creativity in planning your stitchwork.

EVENWEAVE: As the name suggests, evenweave is a specialty fabric woven into an even grid and is usually made of cotton or linen. Like Aida, it comes in lots of beautiful colors, but unlike Aida, it looks like ordinary fabric. Evenweave is used for cross-stitch when Aida is not preferred and is available in minute grid sizes, like 28-count and 32-count. This means the finished project will be much smaller than if it were stitched on standard 14-count Aida. Evenweave can be tricky for novice stitchers and often requires a magnifier or reading glasses to see properly. While experienced stitchers may enjoy using evenweave, for beginners and people looking for a more relaxing experience, we recommend stitching on Aida.

WASTE CANVAS: Waste canvas is a woven fabric grid designed to replicate Aida. Its main use is to create a grid for cross-stitching on any fabric, including felt and denim. Waste canvas is how you would stitch a cross-stitch design onto clothes or home décor items, like tea towels or table runners. To use waste canvas, you will first need to prep your main fabric by placing it in an embroidery snap frame, which pulls it taut. Then you will place the waste canvas atop it and make large basting stitches to secure it in place. (Basting stitches are long single stitches, usually made with ordinary sewing thread, which only serve to hold the waste canvas in place for the duration of your project.) Once you're done cross-stitching, all the basting stitches will be carefully cut away, as well as the waste canvas grid itself. For more thorough instructions, a quick search on the internet will bring up many helpful video tutorials on how to use waste canvas.

Other Tools

TAPESTRY NEEDLE: To cross-stitch you need a tapestry needle. Tapestry needles, when compared to embroidery needles, have a relatively blunt tip. The reason for this is because cross-stitch fabric already has holes in it. Therefore, you don't need a sharp needle to poke through. A size 24 or 26 tapestry needle is recommended for the projects in this book. (Tapestry needles are often sold in variety packs, which allow you to try out different sizes to see what works best for you.)

EMBROIDERY NEEDLE: If you plan on stitching on anything other than Aida or evenweave, you'll need a set of embroidery needles. Unlike tapestry needles, which have a blunt tip, embroidery needles are very sharp and can pierce an array of fabrics, including felt and denim. Buy a pack of embroidery needles in varying lengths and sizes; this way you'll have options on what works best for your project.

NEEDLE MINDER: A needle minder is a small, magnetized accessory designed to hold your needle when you're not stitching. (This prevents it from getting lost or falling on the floor.) It's often made of metal and enamel, like a lapel pin, and comes in all kinds of beautiful shapes and sizes. As with hair ribbons, needle minders serve two purposes—to look cute and to be functional. You can find needle minders at craft stores, needlework shops, and online. Don't be surprised if you end up with a large collection of pretty needle minders! They are, after all, like jewelry for your stitchwork.

THREAD: Six-stranded embroidery floss is the ideal thread for cross-stitch. It comes in hundreds of colors and is easily found at all major craft stores and online. The patterns in this book reference DMC-brand floss colors. (Other brands may be used but be sure to color-match as best you can to the original DMC color.)

EMBROIDERY SCISSORS: Embroidery scissors have a sharp, pointed tip, making them ideal for cutting fine threads. Precision cutting may also be necessary when removing threads if you've made a mistake. Embroidery scissors are also compact, which means they're well suited for stitching on the go.

CRAFT SCISSORS: A quality pair of craft scissors is a must in any crafty circumstance. Cutting Aida and evenweave is made easier with a sharp tip, which minimizes fraying. To keep your craft scissors sharper longer, avoid using them to cut paper.

EMBROIDERY HOOP: An embroidery hoop will always be the simplest way to display completed cross-stitches. Hoops are easy to find at major craft stores and online.

They're available in many sizes, styles, and materials, such as bamboo, birch, and plastic. You may also choose to stitch with an embroidery hoop, although it's not necessary. (In fact, we find it's easier to stitch holding the fabric directly in your hand. Plus, you get to avoid the difficult-to-iron hoop creases in your fabric.) If you're not a fan of the look of natural wood, or you just want to jazz things up, there are lots of neat ways to adorn your embroidery hoop. You can paint it or put glitter on it, as described in "Fun American Girl Cross-Stitch Projects," or you can glue flat-back beads, cabochons, gemstones, or flowers to the outer edge. The possibilities are limited only by your imagination.

NEEDLEWORK SNAP FRAME: This is a kind of embroidery hoop made of thick and sturdy plastic, usually in a square or rectangular shape. It's designed to hold fabric tightly for stitching and comes in handy when stitching on clothing with waste canvas. You will need a snap frame if you're planning on cross-stitching on a jacket or other article of clothing, as described in the "Fun Projects" chapter.

CRAFT GLUE: Craft glue comes in handy for most of the finishing techniques described in this book. (In stitcher's lingo, to "finish" a cross-stitch means to make it ready for display.) There are many brands and varieties of craft glue available but be sure to opt for the liquid variety (avoid glue sticks).

CRAFT FELT: Felt is a thick and soft fabric that's found at all major craft stores and online. It's sold in sheets or by the yard and comes in hundreds of colors. Felt is beloved for its versatility in all kinds of crafts, and its ease of use. The best variety is a wool-acrylic blend, but any variety (all-wool or all-acrylic) will do just fine. You'll need felt to create a few of the projects in the "Fun Projects" chapter.

WOODEN DOWELS: If you're planning on making your cross-stitch into a wall-hanging or banner, you'll need a wooden dowel. Dowels can be found at major craft stores and online, and they come in a variety of diameters and lengths. Choose a size that best

suits your project. For example, you'll need a shorter, thinner dowel for smaller designs like those in the "I'm a(n) . . ." part, or longer dowels with a bigger diameter for projects like "Dreaming of the Stars" or "Rebel with a Hair Ribbon." Learn more about how to determine what you'll need in "Fun American Girl Cross-Stitch Projects."

RIBBON: For any American Girl fan, it goes without saying that ribbons are of critical importance, and for crafting purposes, even more so. Having an array of craft ribbons on hand is always a good thing. Ribbons are versatile and especially useful in projects like hoop art, wall hangings, and banners. For the American Girl projects in this book, choose ribbons that complement the colors and textures of your favorite characters and their time period, such as satin (Samantha), velvet (Rebecca), and gingham (Kirsten). Craft ribbons come in all kinds of sizes; having a variety around will come in handy for all your crafty needs. If you're really looking to have some fun, visit your local craft store. These stores often devote entire aisles to ribbons.

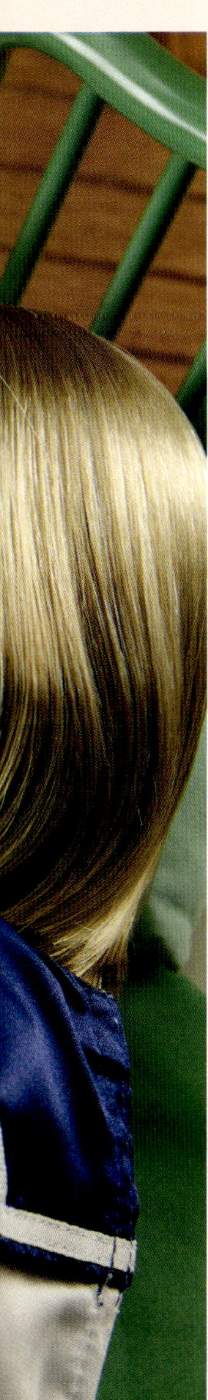

HOW TO READ A CROSS-STITCH CHART

A cross-stitch chart is like a paint-by-numbers chart, but instead of painting, you're making pretty little stitches. Each color block in a cross-stitch chart represents a stitch and corresponds to a particular DMC-brand floss color. Again, you may use any brand of floss you like, so long as you match colors to the original DMC floss.

Read on to learn how to cross-stitch!

How to Cross-Stitch

Before you begin, it's helpful to locate the center of the cross-stitch chart you will be stitching. Then count to the stitch in the farthest right-hand corner of the design, which will be the starting point. Now locate the center of your Aida. Once you know the approximate center, you can count over to the corresponding starting point on the Aida. That's where you make your first stitch.

Prepare your thread by cutting a working length of about 15 inches. (If the thread is longer, it will tangle more easily.) Six-stranded embroidery floss means that the thread can be divided into six individual strands. To cross-stitch, you will use only two strands at a time. Separate two strands from the rest by gently pulling them apart. Do it slowly so the threads don't tangle. Then store the remaining four strands for use later.

Next, load your needle. It helps to snip a bit off your working floss with the embroidery scissors. This gives the thread a crisp edge that will glide more easily through the eye of the needle. Once your needle is loaded, leave a 4- to 5-inch tail on one side. Don't knot your thread!

Cut your Aida to the size specified for each pattern. Give it a gentle run with the iron on the "natural fiber" setting. Now you have a crisp, flat piece of fabric to stitch upon. Remember, you will be holding your Aida fabric directly in hand as you stitch. You may find it comfortable to roll the edge you're holding, like a scroll, as you stitch. Don't worry about gentle hand creases in the fabric—they're easy to iron out later.

TIP: Never apply lotion or hand cream before stitching. The residue will leave stains on your project.

Cross-stitches are done in two parts: the first half cross-stitch, followed by the second half cross-stitch, which creates the charming little X shape. Here's how you begin:

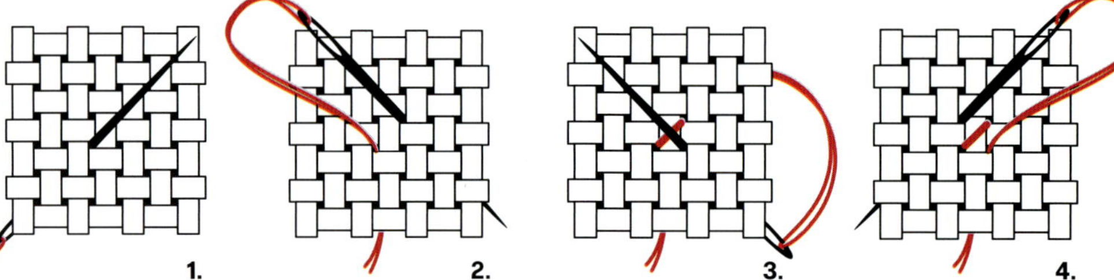

1. Pull your thread up through the small hole at the **BOTTOM LEFT** corner of your starting square, leaving a 1-inch tail of floss on the back of the fabric. (Hold on to that tail as you make your next few stitches right on top of it—you'll want the back side of your stitches to cover the tail, securing it in place.)

2. Pull the thread up through the fabric and then stitch through the **TOP RIGHT** corner of the same square, creating a diagonal stitch. Pull your thread through to the back of the fabric. (Don't pull too tightly, as it will cause the Aida grid to warp. The key to plump and pretty stitches is learning proper stitch tension, which is a balance of not-too-loose and not-too-tight stitches. This takes practice and the building of muscle memory.)

3. Now that you've made the first half of your cross-stitch, stitch up from the back of the Aida through the **BOTTOM RIGHT** corner of the square to the front.

4. Gently tug your thread to make it snug (but not too tight) and cross the square diagonally, stitching down through the **TOP LEFT** hole. You have now created the X shape of your cross-stitch.

TIP: Don't be discouraged if your stitches aren't as pretty as they should be, especially if you're new to the craft of cross-stitch. It takes time to master proper stitch tension. Focus on the art of slowing down and enjoying the process, and your stitchwork will reflect that.

HOW TO CROSS-STITCH IN COLUMNS

The instructions above illustrate how to make cross-stitches individually, but when working with large blocks of the same color, it's more efficient and quicker to make a series of half cross-stitches, and then return to complete them all at once. This technique differs from the one above in how the stitches are assembled. Choose which cross-stitch technique best suits your project.

Working a series of half cross-stitches is best when done in columns and from right to left along the cross-stitch chart. Cross-stitches are done in two parts. First, you will make a series of half cross-stitches, and then you will return to complete each one. Here's how you begin: Start by bringing your needle up through the Aida at point 1 (leaving a 1-inch tail of floss in the back). Bring your needle down to point 2. Come back up at point 3 and back down at point 4. Repeat for the entire column. To complete the cross-stitches, come up at point 9 and go back down at point 10. Then come up at point 11 and go back down at point 12. Repeat until you've completed all the cross-stitches in the column.

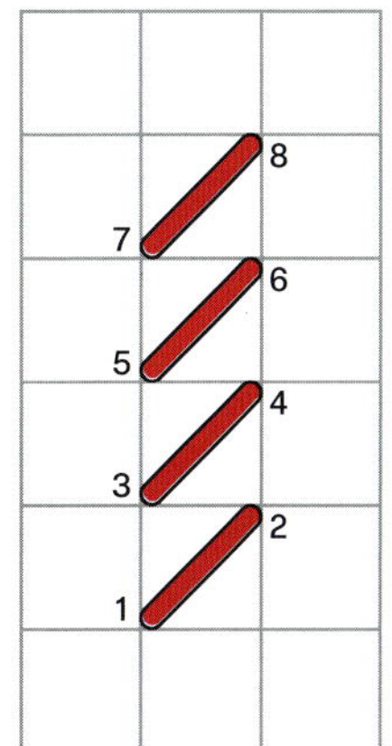

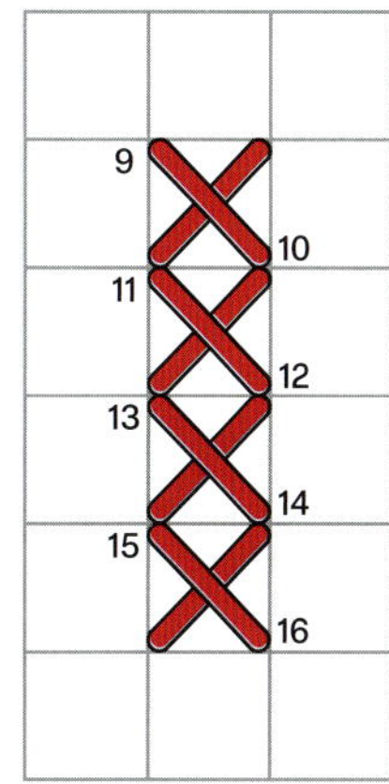

When changing threads or finishing, simply weave the working floss into a few stitches on the back of the Aida and cut.

TIP: Unlike other kinds of embroidery and hand-stitching, in cross-stitch you do not tie off with a knot. All ends are woven into existing stitches for a smooth, flat finish.

HOW TO BACKSTITCH

The intricate outlines you see in the American Girl cross-stitch charts are made using a technique called backstitch. Backstitch adds depth and detail to a design, and it lends a beautiful illustrative vibe to the finished project. Backstitch is a form of freestyle embroidery, wherein you're less interested in being exact and more focused on flow and fun. So, while you should follow the charts closely, it's OK to get creative. The most important thing to remember about backstitch is that it's a *finishing* technique. That means you should never begin backstitching until all your cross-stitches are done. Read on to learn everything you need to know to master this versatile stitch.

For the patterns in this book, use two strands of floss for backstitching. This will result in a thick outline that shows up well against the bold cross-stitch designs.

Before you begin, weave your thread gently into a few stitches in the back of your work to secure it.

Bring your needle up through the fabric at point A, then go back down at point B, and come back up through the bottom at point C. Repeat.

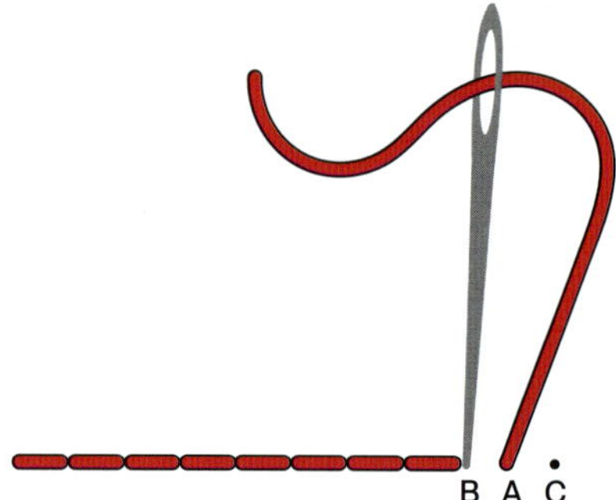

Though it can look daunting, backstitching is quite easy. You can begin anywhere you like; pick a favorite part of the design and follow the chart for stitch placement. Keep in mind that backstitching allows you to "jump" across stitches. That means you can jump across two to six stitches in one unbroken line before going back down into the fabric. This makes for smoother lines and faster stitching. (Try not to jump across more than six stitches, as this will cause your backstitches to "float" and look loose.) It's important to remember to gently tug the thread as you backstitch to make it taut.

TIP: Backstitching is always done last. Once you've made all the cross-stitches in the pattern, that's when you begin to backstitch.

Fun American Girl Cross-Stitch Projects

Cross-stitch is a fun and creative way to express yourself. After stitching your American Girl masterpiece, you're going to want to show it off. Here are some ideas on how to do that, each with a bit of wow factor.

Hoop Art

The best and easiest way to display a finished cross-stitch is in a hoop. Hoops are inexpensive and come in lots of different sizes. You can hang hoop art up on a wall or on a mood board or place it artfully on a shelf or desk—the display possibilities are endless.

DIFFICULTY: Easy

WHAT YOU'LL NEED:

- Embroidery hoop (size depends on your finished cross-stitch)
- Craft scissors
- Small paintbrush
- Craft glue
- White felt sheet large enough to cover the diameter of your hoop
- Twine or ribbon (for hanging the hoop)

Follow these simple steps to hoop your completed American Girl cross-stitch:

1. Iron the finished piece gently on the "natural fiber" setting. Do not iron over the stitches themselves because that will flatten them. Iron along the edge of the design and the main fabric only.

2. Loosen the metal screw on the embroidery hoop. This allows you to separate the inner and outer rings. Place your freshly ironed cross-stitch on top of the inner ring. (Before proceeding, carefully hold it up to the light to make sure your design is centered over the inner ring.) Now place the outer ring over the Aida and inner ring, and firmly press down until it fits snugly. If it looks good, tighten the screw to hold the Aida in place. (If it needs recentering, undo the rings and start again.)

3. Once the design is firmly mounted in the hoop and the screw is tightened, use sharp craft scissors to trim the excess Aida all around the hoop. (Trim as closely to the edge of the hoop as possible.)

4. Now turn your hoop to the back, and using a small paintbrush, apply craft glue all along the outer rim. Place it, glue-side down, onto a large sheet of white felt. Press down firmly to ensure contact. Let dry about 20 minutes.

5. When your hoop and the felt backing are dry, use craft scissors to trim the excess felt from around the hoop. You're now ready to add some twine or ribbon and hang for display.

TIP: Brighten up your hoop art by painting the embroidery hoop first. Acrylic craft paints are ideal for this. Choose a complementary color and paint the outside (larger) hoop only. (The smaller inside hoop can't be seen, anyway.) Let it dry overnight. Then use it as instructed.

No-Sew Throw Pillow

This is a super-easy way to display your masterpiece as home décor, and best of all, no sewing required!

DIFFICULTY: Easy

WHAT YOU'LL NEED:

- Throw pillow
- Craft scissors
- Small paintbrush
- Craft glue

First, choose a favorite throw pillow—one that will match the colors and style of your completed cross-stitch. The size of the pillow should also accommodate the size of the cross-stitch, as you're going to mount the cross-stitch to the center of the throw pillow. Next, carefully iron the completed cross-stitch. Measure roughly 1 inch of space around the cross-stitch design, and carefully cut away the excess Aida. Now pull a few Aida threads upward and off on each side, giving the project a chic frayed border. (The fraying should only be about ¼ inch wide, leaving about ¾ inch of space around the finished design.) Using a small paintbrush, or your fingertips, apply a thin layer of craft glue to the back of the cross-stitch. Eyeball the approximate center of the throw pillow, and gently place the cross-stitch over it, pressing lightly to adhere the cross-stitch to the pillow. Let dry. Spot clean only.

TIP: If you get a knot in your thread, don't panic. (Also, chances are you were stitching too fast.) Some knots can easily be undone, while others require a snip and redo. Stitch more slowly and deliberately to prevent knots.

Wall-Hanging Banner

A wall-hanging banner is a great way to display a cross-stitch. It's clean and modern and suits any décor.

DIFFICULTY: Intermediate

WHAT YOU'LL NEED:

- Felt sheet in a size and color that complements the cross-stitch
- Wooden dowel (size will depend on your finished cross-stitch)
- Craft glue
- Craft scissors
- Sewing pin
- Small paintbrush
- Ribbon (for hanging the banner)

For this project you will need craft felt, a wooden dowel, ribbon, and craft glue. (To learn more about these tools, read "Tools and Techniques.") You can make any finished cross-stitch into a banner. Large or small, it will look wonderful. Simply take your finished cross-stitch and measure a 1-inch border on all sides. Cut the Aida to that border. Carefully pull a few Aida threads upward and out on all sides, giving the edge a frayed effect. (Fray only about ¼ inch of Aida, leaving about ¾ inch of space around your design. This negative space gives your design room to "breathe.") Now iron the Aida carefully on the "natural fiber" setting. Do not press the stitches, as they will flatten. You simply want to remove any visible creases from your cross-stitch. Set aside.

Now, you'll assemble the banner itself. The felt sheet will comprise the main portion of your banner, so choose a color that complements the cross-stitch. If you've read through "Tools and Techniques," you will hopefully have a small selection of wooden dowels. Choose a dowel that will overhang the edge of the banner by about 1 inch. (This depends entirely upon which cross-stitch design you're finishing. For example, if you're making a banner out of one of the "I'm a . . ." designs, the felt and thus the dowel should be smaller and shorter.) Fold the top of the felt sheet over the dowel and glue to the back of the felt. Make sure there's enough room for the dowel to slide back and forth. Let dry. If you choose to do so, you can cut the bottom of the felt into a V shape or into scallops or other decorative edging. That's entirely up to you.

Now, you will carefully place the cross-stitch atop the banner and make sure it's centered. Use a sewing pin to mark its location. With a small paintbrush, paint a thin layer of craft glue on the back side of the cross-stitch. Then place it down onto the felt and press gently to adhere. Let dry at least 4 hours.

As a finishing touch, cut a length of ribbon (length depends on how wide the dowel is and how far you want the banner to hang). Tie the ends of the ribbon to both ends of the dowel, leaving a large loop for hanging.

TIP: Be careful not to use too much glue on the back side of your cross-stitch as it can seep through the holes in the Aida to the front side.

Jacket

Personalizing your favorite jacket is an American tradition. Cross-stitch is a great way to show off not only your favorite American Girl icon or slogan but also your needlecraft skills. The wow factor of this project is off the charts.

DIFFICULTY: Advanced

WHAT YOU'LL NEED:

- Jacket
- Needlework snap frame
- Waste canvas
- Sharp embroidery needle
- Sewing thread
- Craft scissors

For this project you will need a sharp embroidery needle (as opposed to the traditional, blunter tapestry needle when stitching with Aida). You will also need a needlework snap frame and waste canvas, which enables you to cross-stitch on virtually any fabric, including denim. (Waste canvas can be found at all major craft stores and online. See "Tools and Techniques" for more information on how to use waste canvas.) Stretch and secure the back of your jacket in the snap frame. Once it's taut and firmly held in place, secure the waste canvas onto the jacket with a few basting stitches, as described in "Tools and Techniques." Now you're ready to begin stitching. Choose a design that makes a bold statement and fits well on the back of the jacket, such as "Dreaming of the Stars" or "Walk Like an American Girl." Locate the center of the cross-stitch chart, as you normally would, and do the same on the waste canvas. Stitch your design, being careful to glance at the back of your work (the inside of the jacket) periodically, to make sure there aren't any knots or tangles. If your embroidery needle becomes dull, change it out for a fresh one. Once you've finished stitching the design, you will gently pull away the waste canvas threads. (For a closer look on how to do this, look up cross-stitching with waste canvas for tons of helpful videos.)

TIP: If you're planning on cross-stitching on clothing or accessories, consider caring for your finished project by hand-washing or dry-cleaning it. After all, hours of love and stitchwork deserve special treatment.

Greeting Card

Practical and personal, this project is perfect for smaller designs and a great way to share your love of AG with friends, family, and fellow fans. Not only will your greeting card be a thoughtful gift, it will also be a work of art.

DIFFICULTY: Easy

WHAT YOU'LL NEED:

- Blank greeting card or note card in a size that suits your finished cross-stitch
- Craft scissors
- Small paintbrush
- Craft glue

There are many small-scale designs in this book that would be wonderful to stitch for a greeting card. Any of the designs from the "I'm a(n) . . ." part will do. Or choose an element from one of the larger designs in the "AG Life" part, such as the cinnamon roll from "Meet Me at the Café," or one of the hair silhouettes from "Wear It Down" or "Wear It Up," or one of the motifs in "Style Icon." So many fun ideas!

Once you've stitched the design, give it a gentle run with the iron. Then measure a 1-inch border around the design, and trim away any excess Aida. Carefully pull a few Aida threads upward and out on all sides, giving the edge a frayed effect. (Fray only about ¼ inch of Aida, leaving about ¾ inch of space around your design.) Now is the time to decide whether your cross-stitch looks better on a card horizontally or vertically, and orient the card based on that. Using the paintbrush, apply a thin layer of craft glue to the back side of your cross-stitch. Roughly center the cross-stitch on the front of the greeting card and press down to adhere. Let dry overnight. Your recipient will be thrilled with your adorable card!

TIP: Proper stitch tension is the difference between plump and pretty cross-stitches or stitches that look too tight and rigid. Proper stitch tension requires slowing down and being in the moment. A great way to do that is to take a few deep, calming breaths before a stitch session.

Framed Art

Sometimes the best way to display a finished cross-stitch is simply to frame it. Framing adds a touch of class to the overall design, as well as lending a bit of grandeur to it.

DIFFICULTY: Intermediate

WHAT YOU'LL NEED:

- A picture frame in a size suited to your finished cross-stitch, including its cardboard insert
- Craft glue
- Craft scissors
- Masking tape

For this project you'll need a picture frame, a cardboard insert, craft glue, and a sharp pair of craft scissors. Choose a frame that suits the size of your finished cross-stitch.

Note: It's up to you whether you wish to use the glass or not, but we recommend doing without it. Glass adds glare, and what's worse, it will flatten your stitches. Also, cross-stitch is a tactile craft, and glass obscures details that would otherwise be visible. Think of it this way—fine art paintings are almost always framed *without* glass. Your finished cross-stitch is every bit as special.

To prepare your cross-stitch for framing, give it a gentle run with the iron on the "natural fiber" setting, being careful not to flatten your stitches by pressing too hard. Next, place the crisply ironed Aida over the cardboard frame insert, holding it up to a light to center your design. Once it's roughly centered, gently lift the corners, one at a time, and apply a small dab of craft glue to the cardboard insert. Press the Aida firmly down to adhere. Once all four corners of the cardboard insert have adhered to the back of the finished cross-stitch, let dry for about 1 hour. (At this point you will have lots of Aida overhang on all sides.) Once everything has dried, turn the cardboard insert over, Aida side down, and gently fold the excess Aida to the back, trimming as necessary to reduce fabric bulk. Fold in the corners as you would wrap a present, and use masking tape to secure the fabric to the cardboard. Where the fabric meets itself at the corners, use craft glue to secure together.

Alternately, once you've centered and glued the cross-stitch to the front of the cardboard insert, you can simply cut away the excess Aida that surrounds it. The frame will cover any uneven edges. You'll have a beautiful American Girl display piece to adorn any room or to give as a gift.

TIP: One of the easiest ways to get discouraged from regular crafting is not being able to find your supplies. Craft supply boxes come in myriad shapes and sizes and make it easy to store your cross-stitch tools for future use. Best of all, they can be decorated and customized.

Ornaments

Ornaments are a great way to display your American Girl cross-stitch during the holidays—or any time! Choose smaller designs, or pluck a single motif from a larger design, such as Maryellen's necklace from "Style Icon," or Coconut the dog (or Licorice the cat!) from "Besties."

DIFFICULTY: Easy

WHAT YOU'LL NEED:

- Felt sheets
- Craft glue
- Small paintbrush
- Embroidery hoop
- Twine or ribbon (for hanging)
- Glitter

FESTIVE HOOP ART

There's more than one way to make a pretty ornament, and the first is simply to hoop it. Follow the instructions above in "Hoop Art" to turn your cross-stitch into an adorable ornament fit for displaying anytime. Be sure to jazz it up with some pretty twine or sparkly ribbon for hanging. And if you want to go all-out in your festive display, add some glitter! Simply paint a thin coat of craft glue to the outer rim of the outer hoop (embroidery hoops always include the large outer hoop and small inner hoop, which cannot be seen in the finished display). Sprinkle some glitter on a paper plate and roll the edge of the hoop in the glitter to coat evenly. Let dry overnight. Then use the hoop as instructed to create your ornament.

TIP: **As you cross-stitch, your thread will become tangled over time. It's good to occasionally let your needle and thread drop (like a plumb bob) to untwist itself. You'll be surprised at the number of times it may spin. Doing this periodically keeps your thread tension-free, which makes for prettier stitches.**

FELT ORNAMENTS

Felt ornaments are another wonderful way to display your finished American Girl cross-stitch. The best part is they double as gift tags. (Coupled with a pretty bow, cross-stitch gift tags look amazing on Christmas, birthday, or anytime gifts.) Once your cross-stitch is complete, measure about ½ inch from the edge of the design and cut away the excess with a sharp pair of craft scissors. Gently pull away two to three strands of Aida from all sides to fray the edges of the cross-stitch. Now, place your cross-stitch atop a sheet of felt, measuring about a ½-inch border on all sides. Trim the excess felt away. Using a paintbrush, brush a thin layer of craft glue to the back side of the cross-stitch, center it on the piece of felt, and press down to adhere. Let dry 1 hour. Snip a tiny hole near the top of the felt and insert ribbon or twine for hanging.

Hand Towels

Since time immemorial, stitchers have been finding clever ways to make their art more functional. Hand towels are a cross-stitch tradition, and now you can make one-of-a-kind American Girl hand towels for yourself or as gifts.

DIFFICULTY: Easy

WHAT YOU'LL NEED:

- Charles Craft velour 14-count hand towel
- Tapestry needle
- Thread
- Needlework snap frame
- Craft scissors

Cross-stitch hand towels have a premade Aida-like grid for stitching. Use the grid as you would ordinary Aida. Find the approximate center of the towel grid, and stitch as normal. Hand towels are also a great way to embrace the art of repeats. That means taking a smallish design and repeating it side by side all along the width of the towel. You can do this with any of the smaller designs in this book, such as the stars from "Dreaming of the Stars," or the hair silhouettes from "Wear It Down" and "Wear It Up." With cross-stitch towels, you're only limited by the amount of grid space afforded by the towel manufacturer.

TIP: **Wash your hands before stitching. This will keep your stitchwork looking clean and pretty. You can use your new AG hand towel to dry your hands!**

Part One: Iconic American Girl

Few symbols of childhood are as powerful or memorable as the classic American Girl logo and star. They evoke feelings of warmth and belonging, much the same way the characters and their stories do. Stitch these two designs for yourself or make them for a friend and share the bond that only comes from being an American Girl fan.

TIP: Cross-stitch is aces at helping you slow down. Embrace it. Lock up your phone for an hour, grab your favorite American Girl doll, and sit down together for a magical and relaxing stitch session.

American Girl Logo

The American Girl logo is truly iconic. Its bold and timeless design is instantly recognizable. Stitch it for yourself or a fellow fan, display it proudly, and leave no doubt you're a part of the ever-growing American Girl fandom.

DIFFICULTY: Easy

■ DMC-310 ▬ DMC-310

Finished size on 14-count Aida: 3" x 3"

Approximate stitch time: 4–6 hours

Aida fabric size: 7" x 7"

Display hoop size: 5–6" hoop

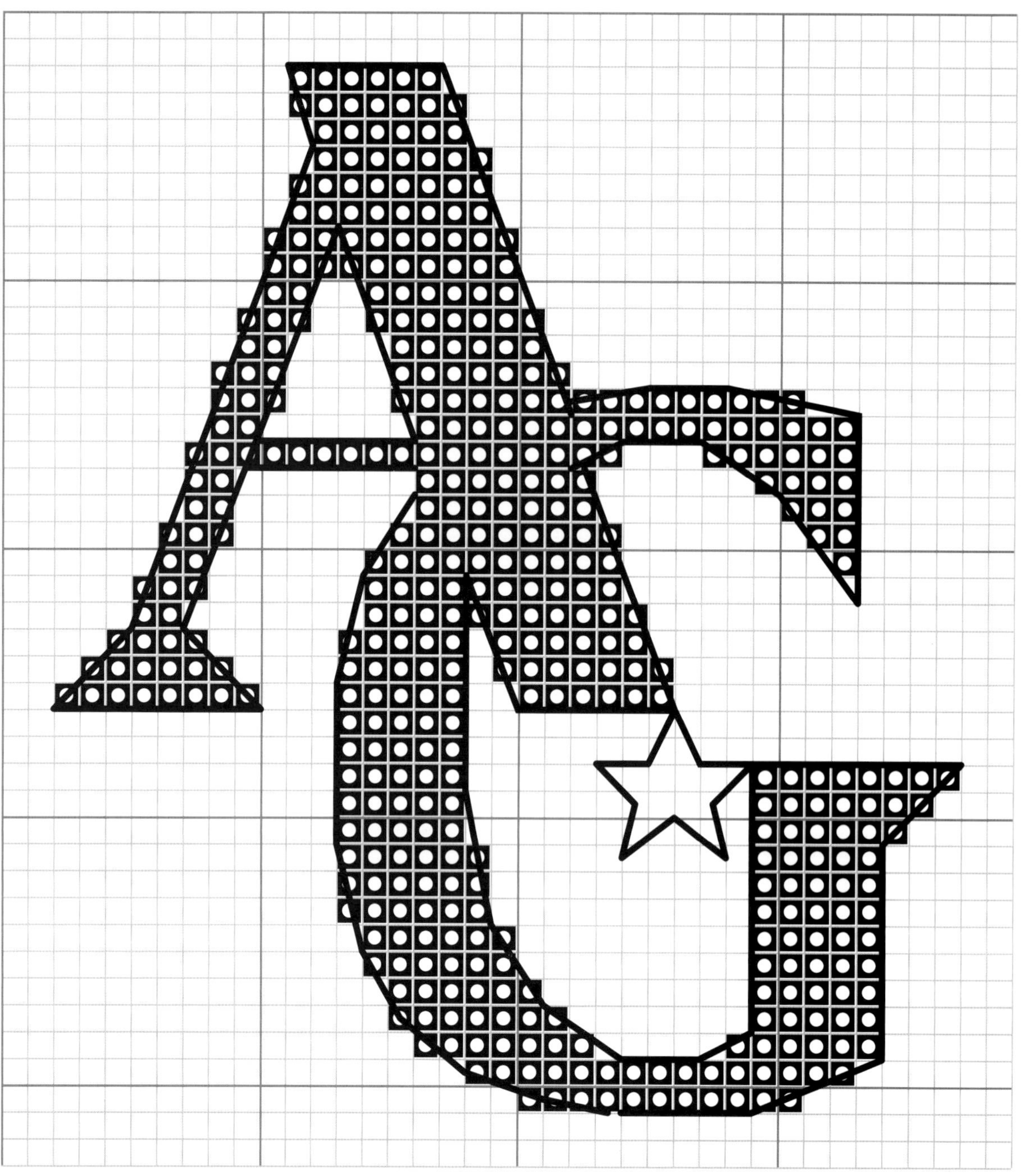

Legend:
DMC-310

Backstitches:
DMC-310

AG

American Girl Classic Star

If American Girl helped you find your inner star, then let it shine. Stitch this striking symbol of girlhood's bravery on the back of a jean jacket or turn it into hoop art for display at home or at work. The classic star is truly a symbol of all that is berry and true.

DIFFICULTY: Easy

DMC-600 DMC-600

Finished size on 14-count Aida: 5" x 5"
Approximate stitch time: 4–6 hours
Aida fabric size: 9" x 9"
Display hoop size: 6–7" hoop

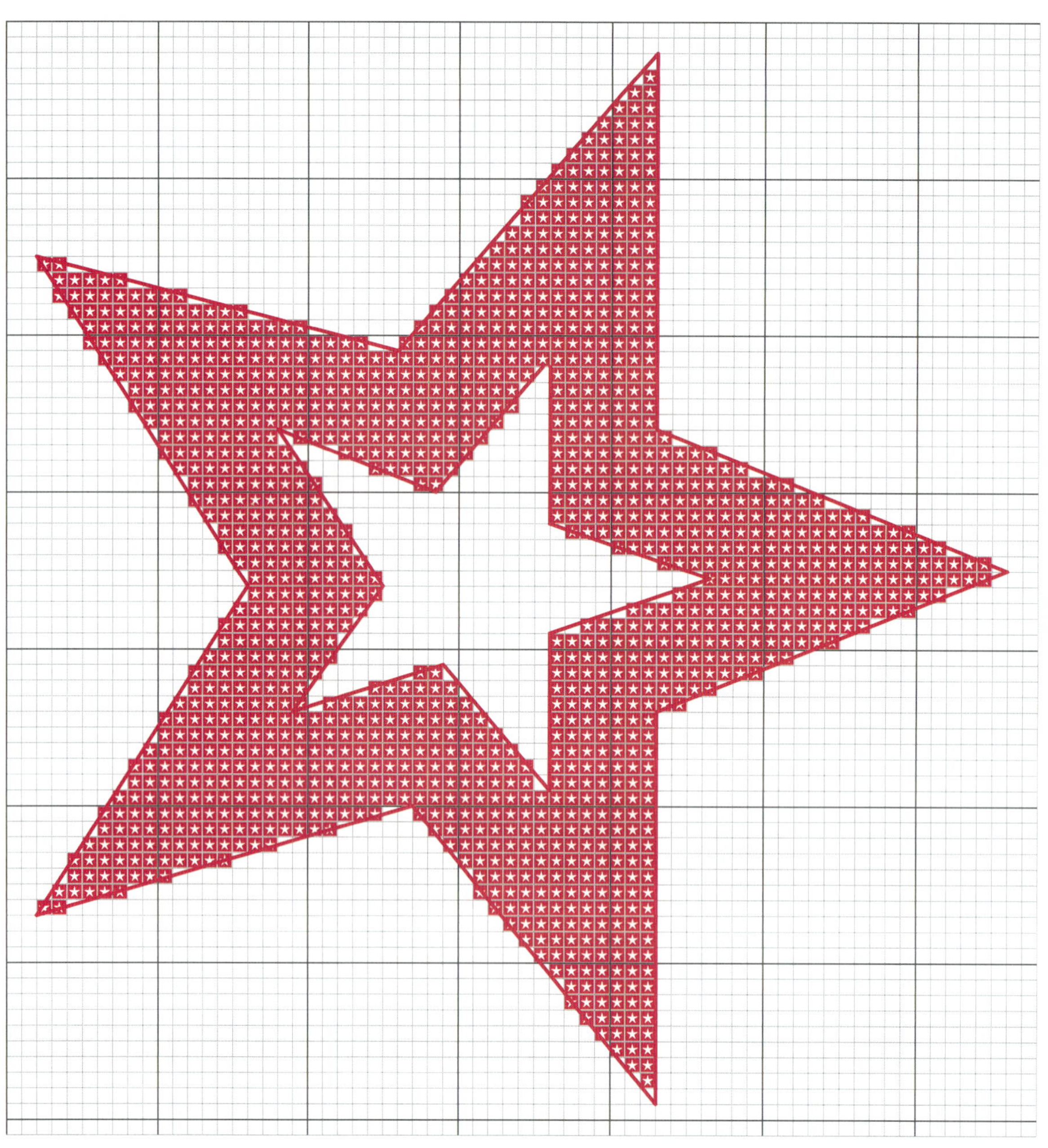

Legend:

DMC-600

Backstitches:

DMC-600

Part Two: I'm a . . .

Part of the enduring bond between American Girl dolls and their grown-up human incarnations is their mutual relatability. The Historical Characters provided, through stories and play, a way of connecting the past to the present. Girlhood through time and space, not surprisingly, remains constant.

Each of the following designs is a representation of a Historical Character, featuring one of her iconic pieces of clothing or accessories. Stitch the designs individually or make a larger, bolder statement by combining them with the "I'm a . . ." cross-stitch pattern.

TIP: **Cross-stitch is about having fun. If a project gets too "real," it's time to pause and take a breath. It's OK to take days, weeks, or even months to complete a cross-stitch, as long as you're enjoying yourself.**

I'm a(n) . . .

DIFFICULTY: Intermediate

■	DMC-310	—	DMC-310
■	DMC-600	—	DMC-600

Finished size on 14-count Aida: 13" x 5" (12" x 5")
Approximate stitch time: 7–8 hours plus individual character cross-stitch
Aida fabric size: 17" x 9 " (16" x 9")
Display hoop size will vary.

To customize your "I'm a(n) . . ." cross-stitch, choose one of the patterns below and cut your Aida to the recommended size. Next, choose your character—the one that most connects with or resembles you on some level. (Maybe it's something as simple as being the only girl in class who wore glasses that connects you to Molly. Or maybe it's Julie's drive to become the first girl on a team full of boys that reminds you of your own inner drive to remove barriers and level the playing field.)

Once you've chosen your fav character, note the center point on her chart. Now note the small berry-colored square on the "I'm a . . ." chart. Those two center points coincide. Begin stitching based off that location. For the "I'm a(n) . . ." design, we have already provided the chart in combination with Addy's necklace (as "I'm an . . ." only applies to Addy).

TIP: Start by stitching the character chart first, moving through the overall design from right to left. That way even if you miscount stitch placement, you'll always have room on your Aida to complete the overall design.

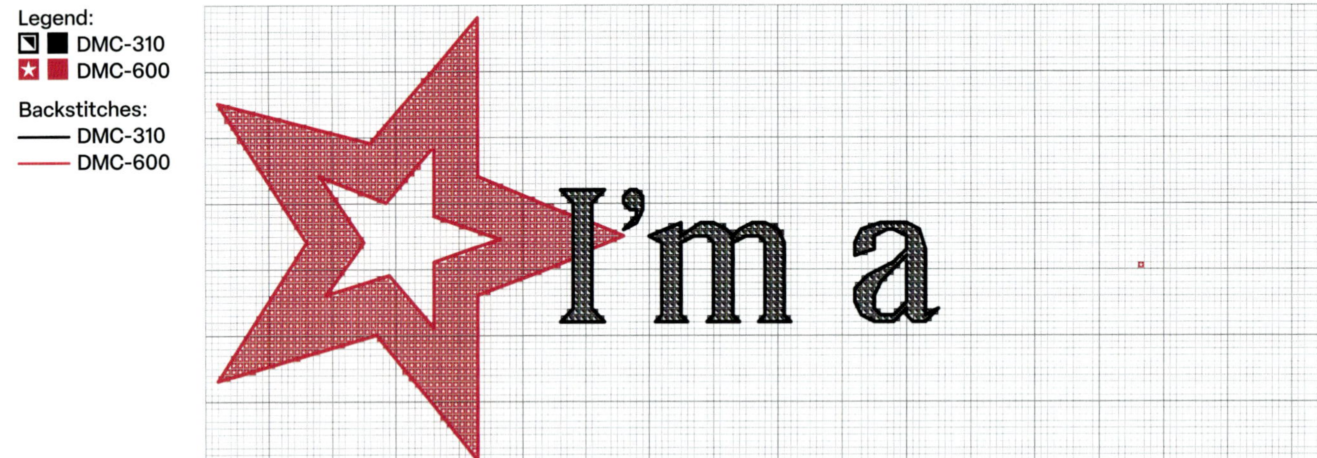
Legend:
DMC-310
DMC-600
Backstitches:
DMC-310
DMC-600
I'm a

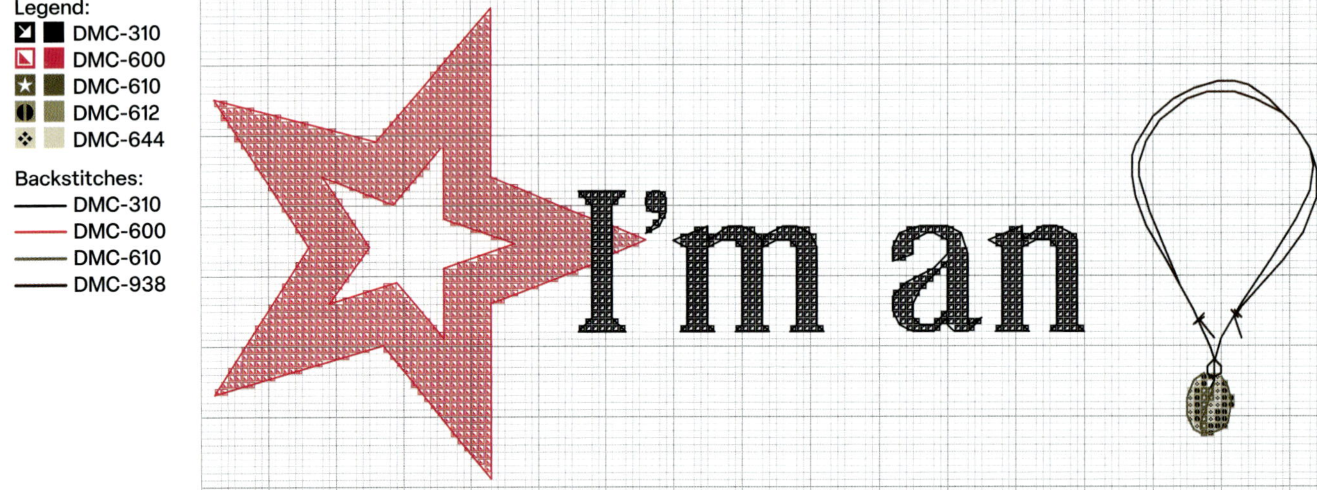
Legend:
DMC-310
DMC-600
DMC-610
DMC-612
DMC-644
Backstitches:
DMC-310
DMC-600
DMC-610
DMC-938
I'm an

I'm a
I'm an

Molly

Braided and bespectacled and donning a blue beret, Molly is ready to take the world by storm, one act of patriotism at a time. A leader at heart, she knows how to stir up kindness and compassion in others and knows when to lend a hand during difficult times. Although the adult realities and world events may force her to confront grown-up challenges at an early age, she stays in good spirits and finds a way to do her part—along with the help of friends and her adorable dog, Bennett, of course!

DIFFICULTY: Easy

DMC-803
DMC-823
DMC-823

Finished size on 14-count Aida: 3.5" x 3"
Approximate stitch time: 4–6 hours
Aida fabric size: 8" x 8"
Display hoop size: 6–7" hoop

DOLL DEETS

Molly McIntire lends a hand on the home front during World War II. She misses her father, who's a doctor overseas tending to soldiers during the war. She is a great tap dancer, dreads multiplication, dislikes turnips, and loves to go to Camp Gowonagin.

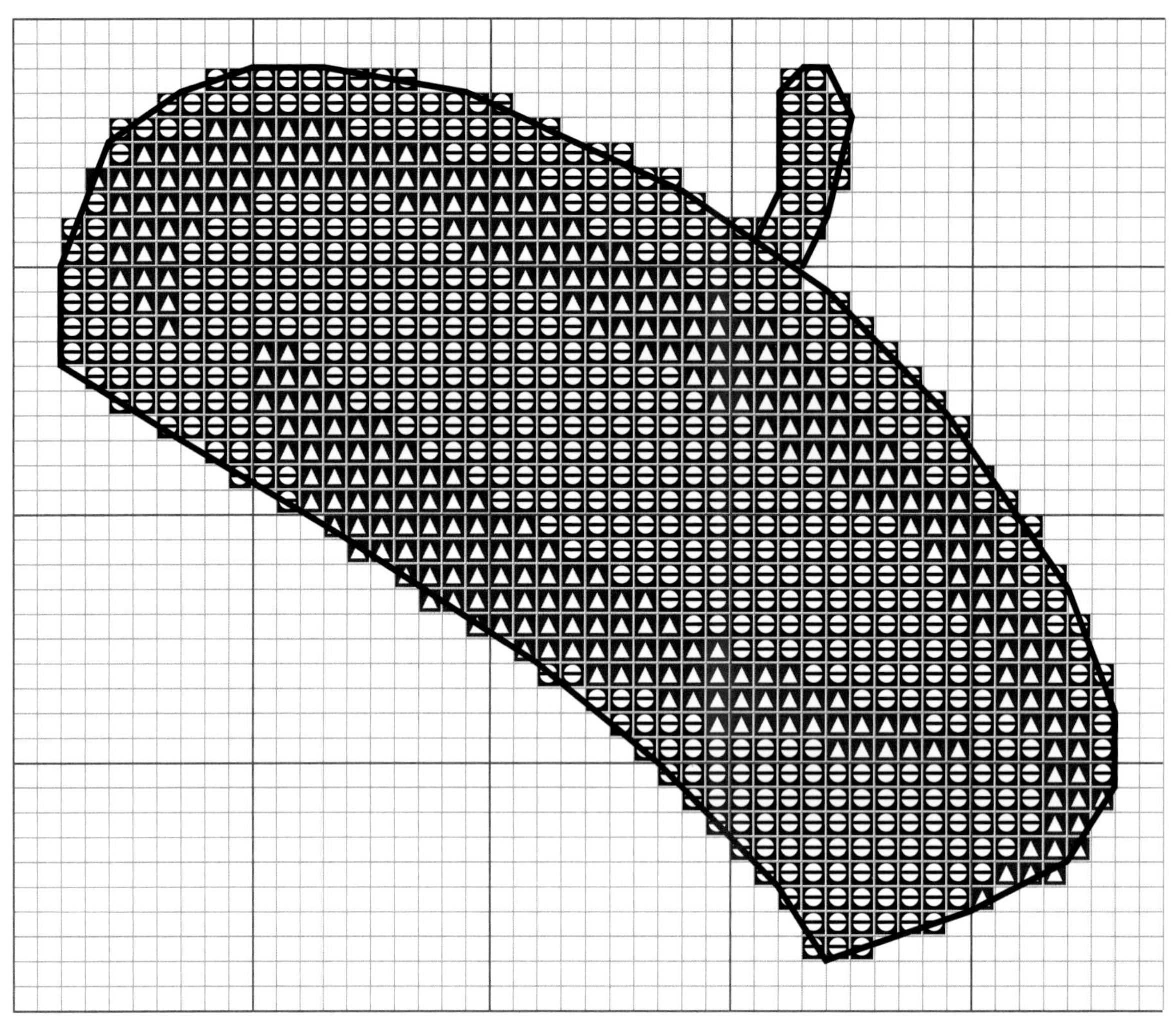

Legend:
DMC-803
DMC-823

Backstitches:
DMC-823

Kirsten

The Minnesota prairie is a challenging place for a girl to grow up in pioneer times, to say the least. Fortunately, Kirsten is a courageous American Girl. Wearing a bonnet and filled with unwavering curiosity, Kirsten teaches us that while the old and the new can sometimes clash, they can also join to create a stronger, more resilient renewed version of yourself. Braided and brave, Kirsten is ready to take on whatever comes her way—bears and snowstorms included!

DIFFICULTY: Intermediate

DMC-349
DMC-351
DMC-816

Finished size on 14-count Aida: 3.5" x 4"
Approximate stitch time: 6–7 hours
Aida fabric size: 8" x 8"
Display hoop size: 6–7" hoop

DOLL DEETS

Kirsten Larson is a pioneer of strength and spirit, growing up on the Minnesota prairie in 1854, when many Europeans and people from the East Coast settled in the Midwest. Kirsten was born in Ryd, Sweden, and initially finds it difficult to fit in to her new home in Minnesota. She loves to bake Swedish treats and gradually learns to be less homesick, making new friends, learning new things, and spending time with her family.

1854
K. L.

Legend:
DMC-349
DMC-351
Backstitches:
DMC-816

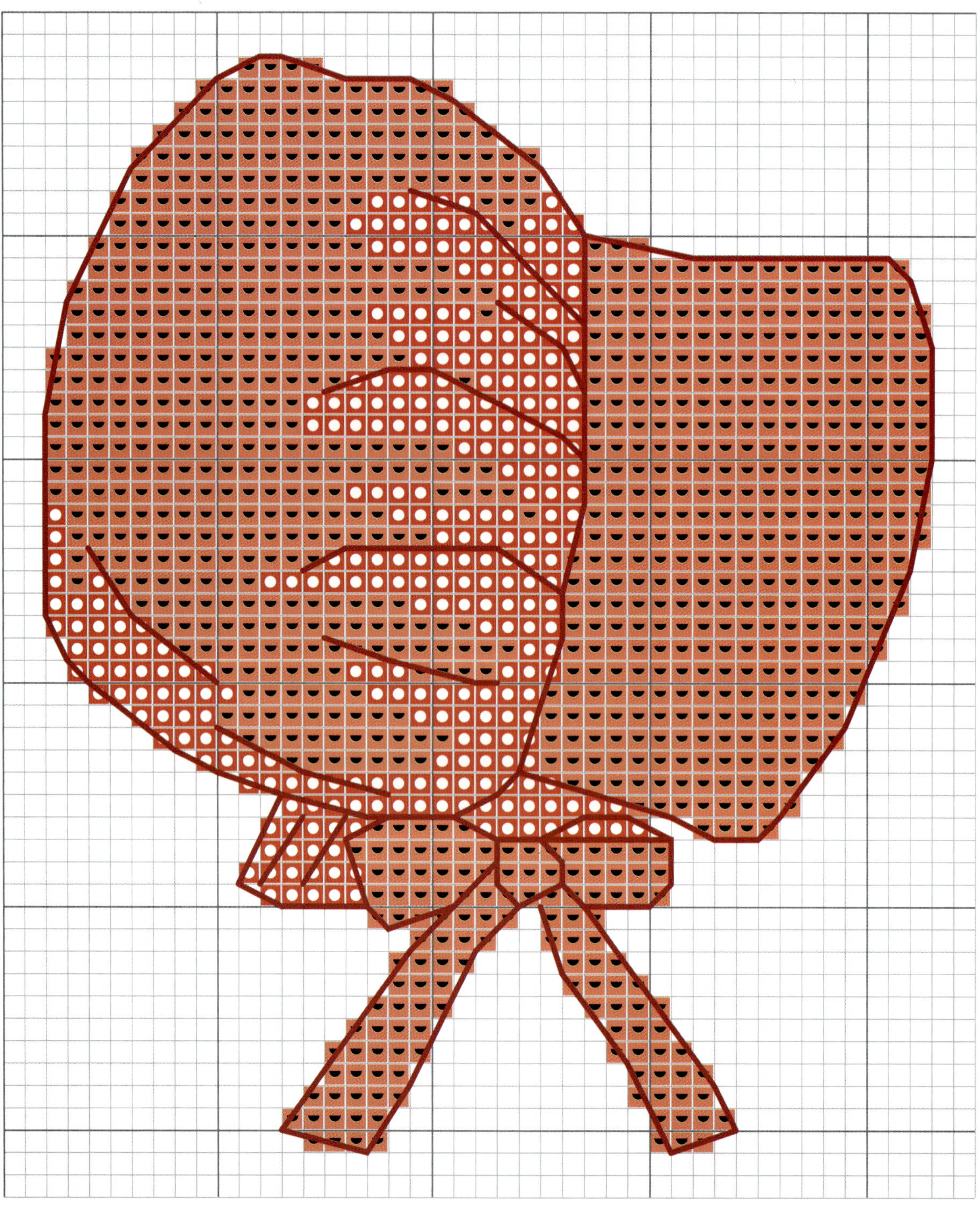

Addy

Addy's story is one of great courage and love—love of family and love of freedom. Her unshakable belief in her family and freedom is a powerful light to shine on racism, prejudice, and hate in her time—and today. Her necklace is not only charming, but it also carries great meaning for Addy. On it hangs a cowrie shell, brought from Africa by her great-grandmother, Aduke ("much loved"), who she's named after.

DIFFICULTY: Easy

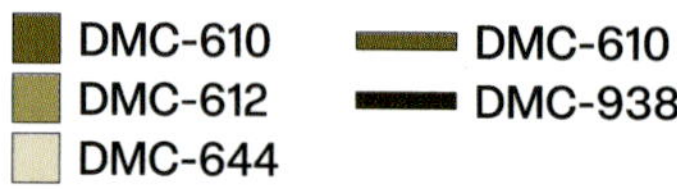

Finished size on 14-count Aida: 2.5" x 4"
Approximate stitch time: 2–3 hours
Aida fabric size: 8" x 8"
Display hoop size: 6–7" hoop

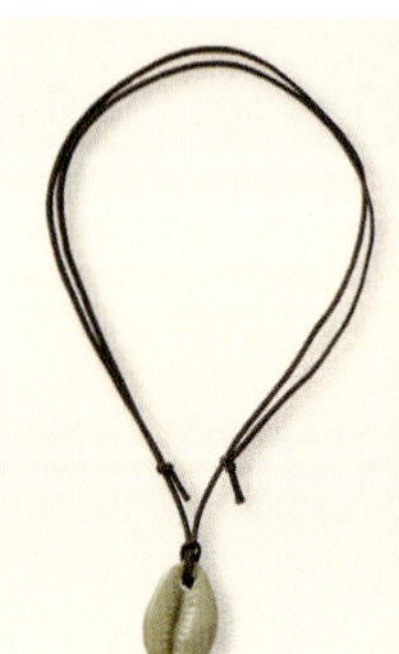

DOLL DEETS
Addy Walker is a courageous girl determined to be free in the midst of the Civil War. In 1864, Addy's poppa and brother are sold to another plantation, and she and her momma escape to Philadelphia. Over the course of her stories, Addy and her family are reunited, but the war has changed them all. As Uncle Solomon once told Addy, freedom has a cost. Her dream is to become a teacher, and her hobbies include making puppets and putting on puppet shows.

Legend:

- ★ DMC-610
- › DMC-612
- + DMC-644

Backstitches:

- DMC-610
- DMC-938

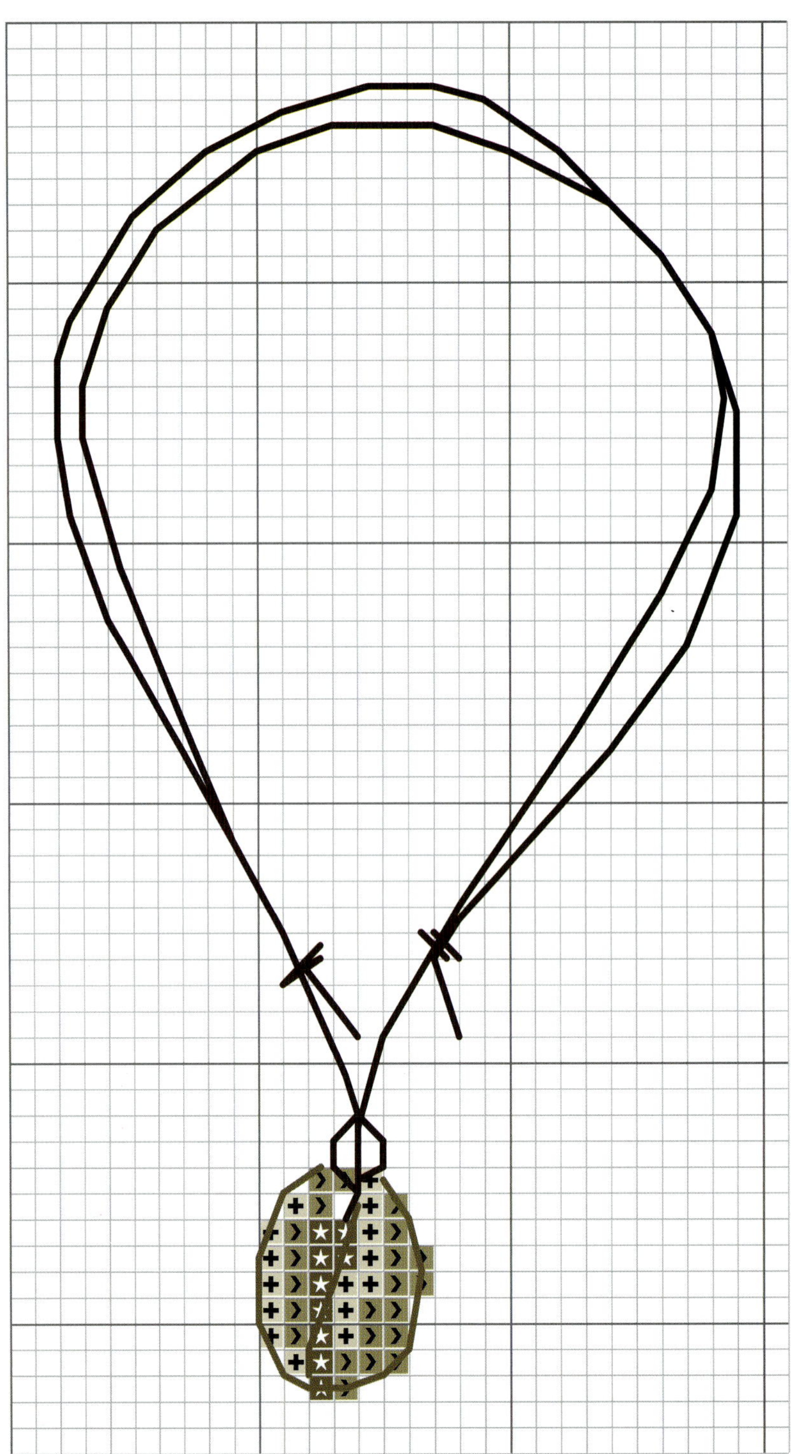

Rebecca

To fit in or to stand out in the crowd? That is the question. Rebecca faces this struggle, reminding us that the things that make us different (read: unique) are often our most interesting qualities. Whatever your talent or interest or background, let it shine!

DIFFICULTY: Intermediate

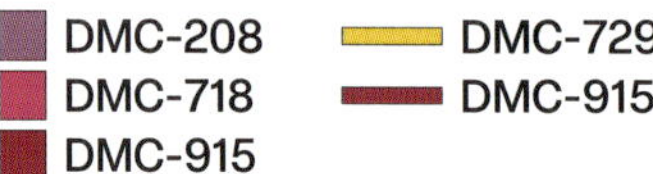

Finished size on 14-count Aida: 4" x 2.5"

Approximate stitch time: 7–8 hours

Aida fabric size: 8" x 8"

Display hoop size: 6–7" hoop

DOLL DEETS

Charismatic Rebecca Rubin's year is 1914. She balances Jewish traditions with new American ideas—like becoming an actress in the movies! Through this internal struggle, she finds her way. Rebecca's a natural at math and business and even has a crafty side with a love for crocheting.

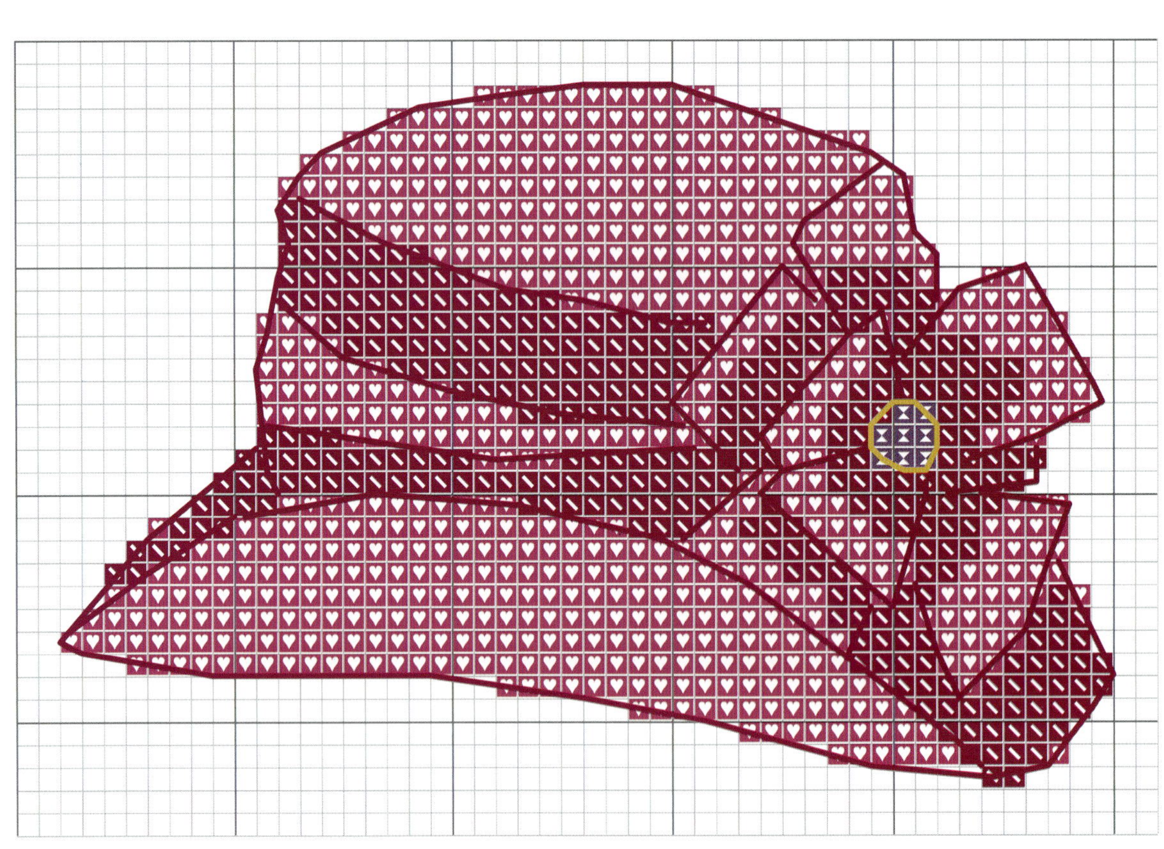

Legend:

- DMC-208
- DMC-718
- DMC-915

Backstitches:

- DMC-729
- DMC-915

Samantha

Samantha wears the bow that launched a thousand dreams. Many references to American Girl invariably include some version of this hair ribbon, and we have her to thank. Samantha's one of the original three American Girl Historical Characters launched by the original Pleasant Company in 1986. Her generosity of spirit, kindness, and compassion have made her beloved by fans across generations.

DIFFICULTY: Easy

DMC-347
DMC-815
DMC-815

Finished size on 14-count Aida: 4" x 3"
Approximate stitch time: 5–6 hours
Aida fabric size: 8" x 8"
Display hoop size: 6–7" hoop

DOLL DEETS

Samantha Parkington's year is 1904, during the Victorian era and the turn of the twentieth century. She walks the path between the more conservative ideas of her grandmother, Grandmary, and her aunt Cornelia's progressive ones, finding her own way to being "a proper young lady." Samantha's favorite book is *The Wonderful Wizard of Oz*, which was popular during this time, and she enjoys spending time outdoors.

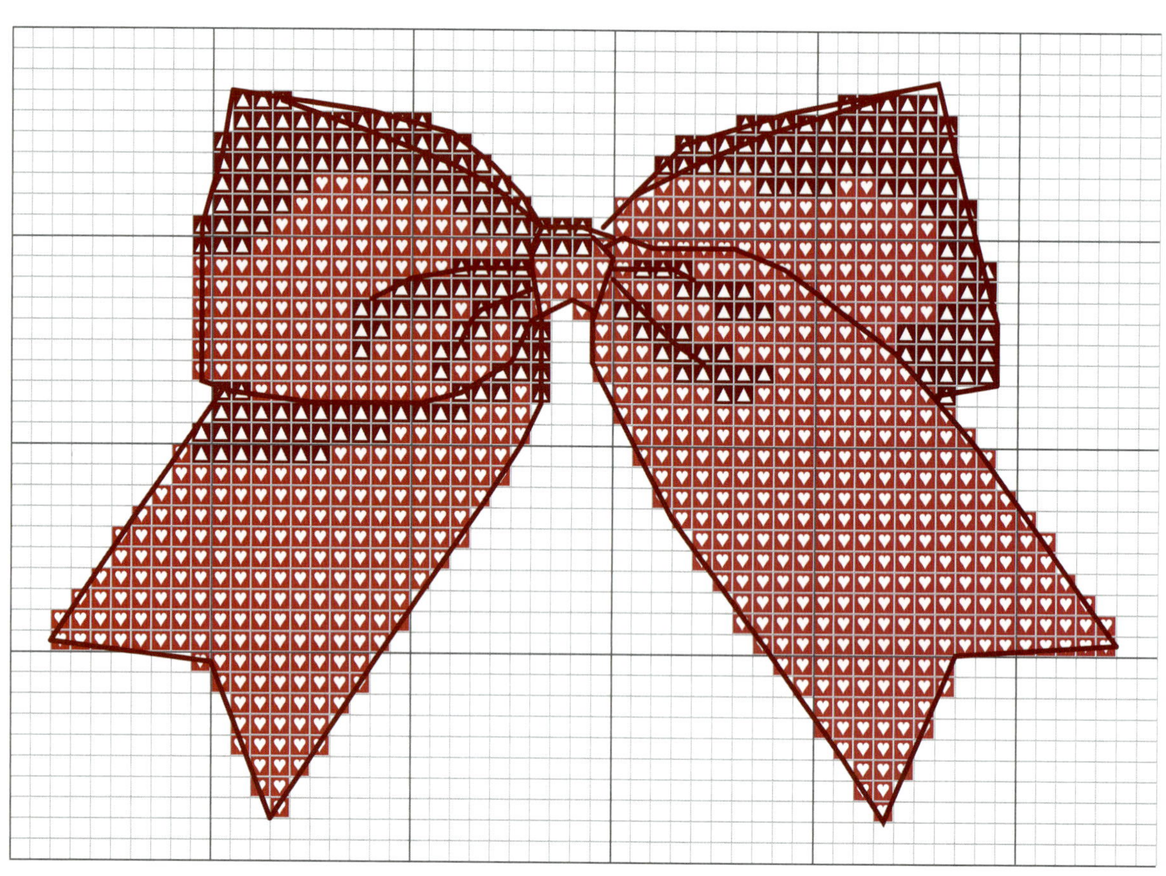

Legend:

♥ ■ DMC-347

△ ■ DMC-815

Backstitches:

—— DMC-815

Maryellen

In an era where conformity was the norm, Maryellen teaches us the meaning of true originality. She loves her poodle skirt and rocket science, too, and sees no reason not to be fashionable while showing the boys how to defy gravity. Both things could be true at the same time! Maryellen reminds us to challenge those who try to define us.

DIFFICULTY: Advanced

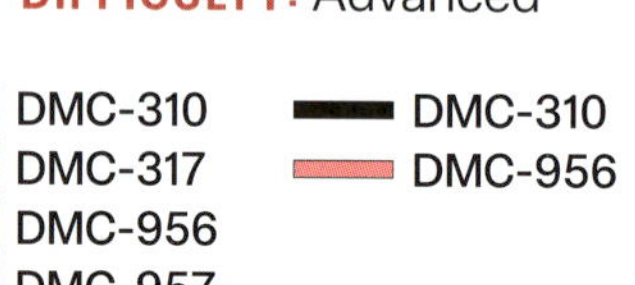

Finished size on 14-count Aida: 4" x 3"
Approximate stitch time: 6–7 hours
Aida fabric size: 8" x 8"
Display hoop size: 6–7" hoop

DOLL DEETS

Maryellen Larkin's year is 1954, when television shows like *The Lone Ranger* and *Davy Crockett* were all the rage (and Maryellen's favs, btw). She caught polio when she was seven, resulting in a weak leg, but that never stopped Maryellen from running, swimming, and ice skating. It also increased her interests in medicine and science.

Seaside Diner
A3 Let's Stroll
C1 One Glass, Two Straws
E1 Sweetheart Serenade
C5 Soda Shop Hop
E3 Beachside Boogie
A5 Ice Cream Dreams
A B C D E
1 2 3 4 5

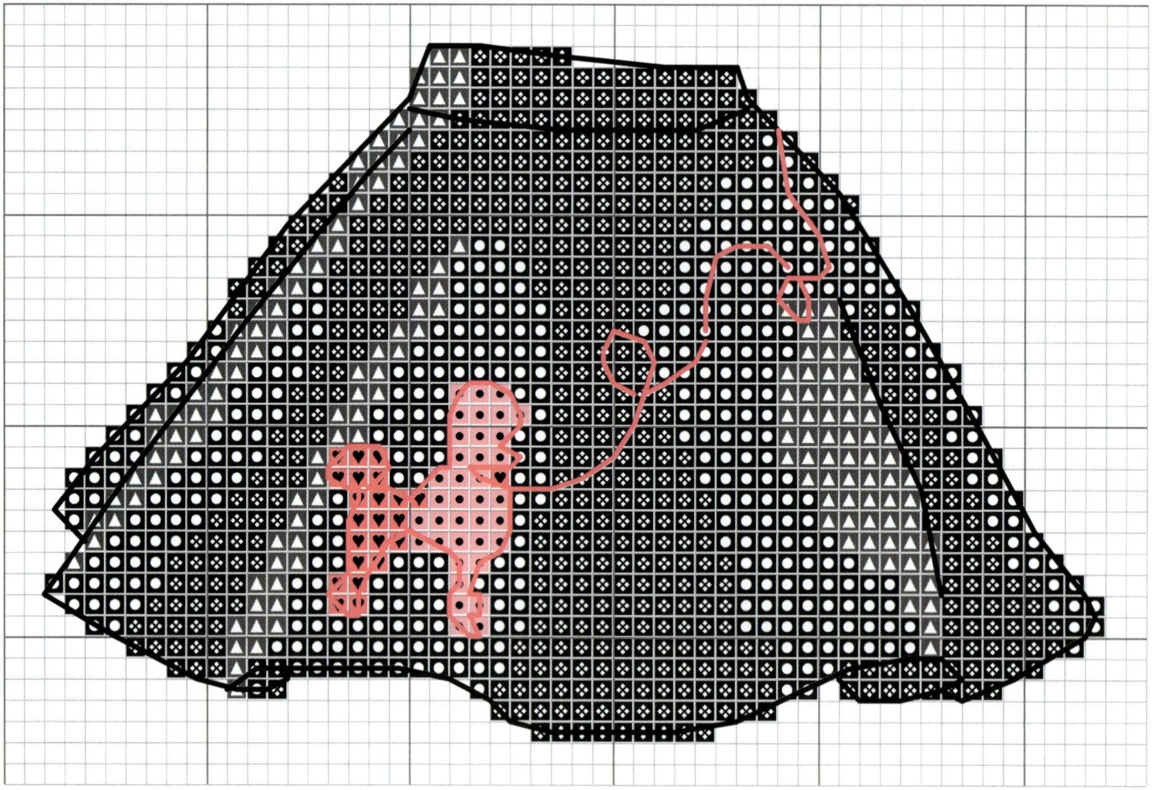

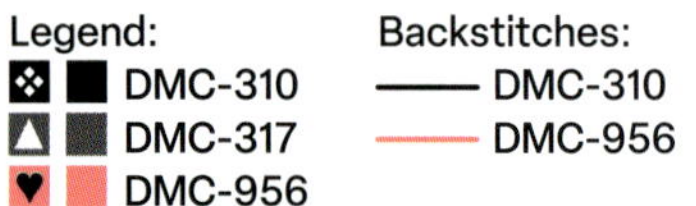
Legend:
DMC-310
DMC-317
DMC-956
DMC-957
DMC-3799
Backstitches:
DMC-310
DMC-956

Kaya

Kaya longs to be a bold, courageous leader for her people, the Niimíipuu. In her belt pouch she carries all she needs to succeed in most any situation—even a courageous escape from enemies! Riding out the storm bears new meaning for the original horse girl, in her quest for self-confidence and discovery.

DIFFICULTY: Advanced

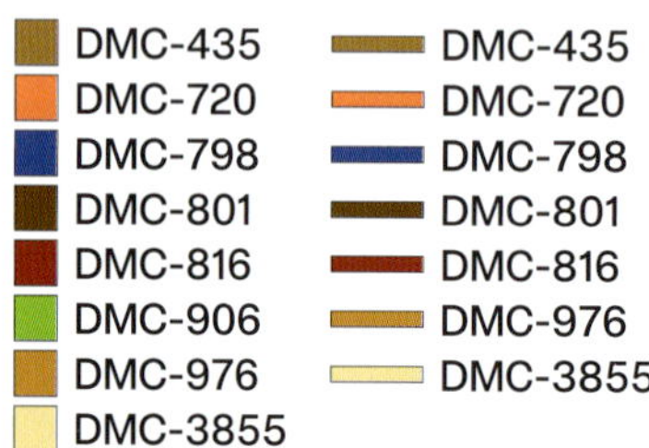

Finished size on 14-count Aida: 3" x 4"

Approximate stitch time: 6–7 hours

Aida fabric size: 8" x 8"

Display hoop size: 6–7" hoop

DOLL DEETS

Kaya's year is 1764, making her the first American Girl. She loves nothing better than to ride her beautiful, spirited Appaloosa mare through her homeland in present-day Idaho, Washington, and Oregon. She deeply cares for her family, and she lives in tune with nature, keeping her world a safe and beautiful place for future generations.

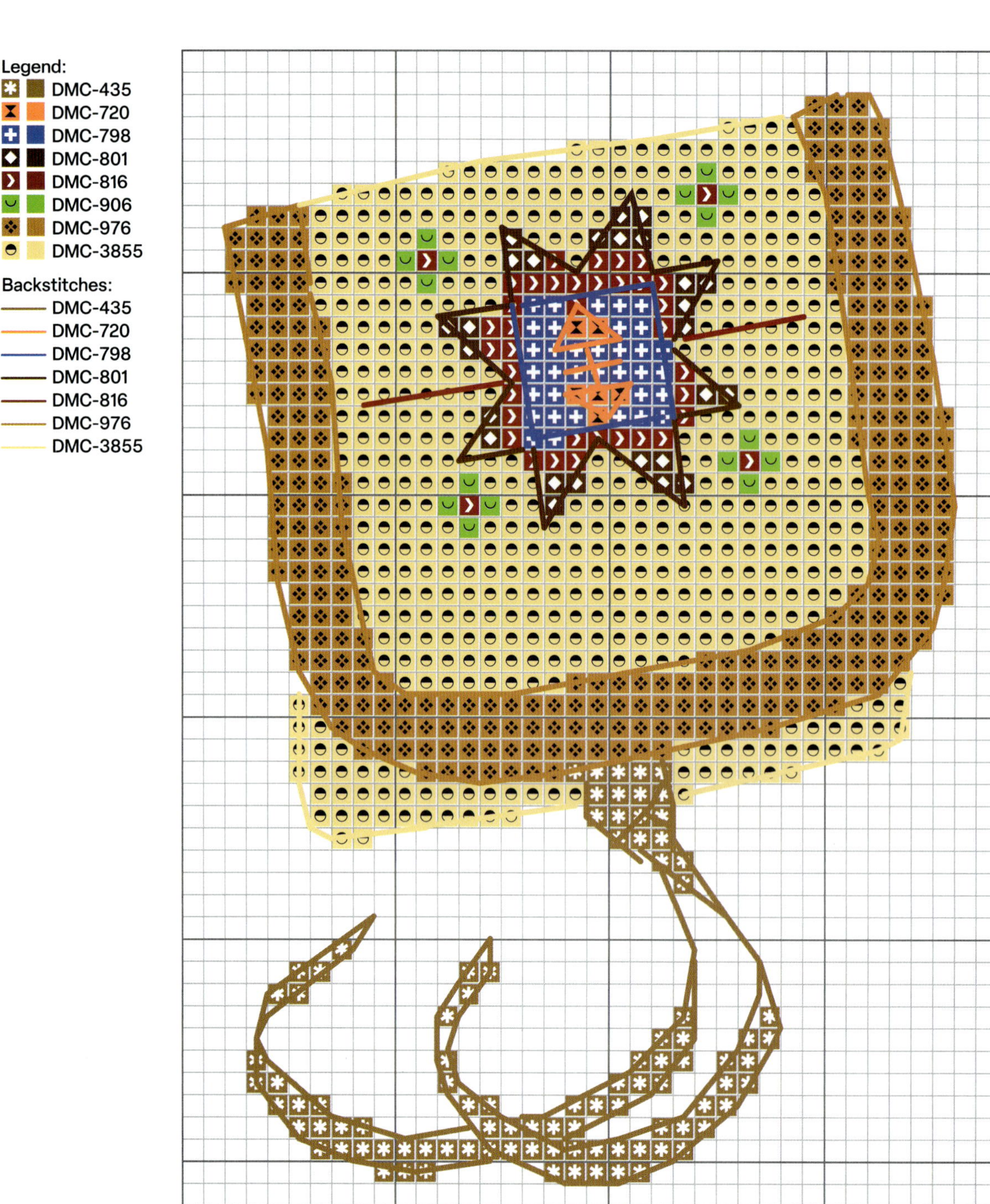
Legend:
DMC-435
DMC-720
DMC-798
DMC-801
DMC-816
DMC-906
DMC-976
DMC-3855
Backstitches:
DMC-435
DMC-720
DMC-798
DMC-801
DMC-816
DMC-976
DMC-3855

Kit

When times are tough, Kit gets tougher. Independent to a fault, she's a natural do-it-yourself type. Inquisitive and earnest, Kit embodies the strength in all of us to face life's challenges with a greater sense of purpose. Adventurous, she loves playing outside and writing stories of happenings around the neighborhood—all while rocking her bob and sweet white-knit cap.

DIFFICULTY: Intermediate

- DMC-677
- DMC-704
- DMC-746
- DMC-3348
- DMC-677 (line)
- DMC-704 (line)

Finished size on 14-count Aida: 4" x 3"

Approximate stitch time: 6–7 hours

Aida fabric size: 8" x 8"

Display hoop size: 6–7" hoop

DOLL DEETS

In 1934, Kit Kittredge faces the Great Depression with grit and determination. She has a basset hound named Grace, and her dream is to become a newspaper reporter. Kit writes her own newspaper for her friends and family called *The Hard Times News*.

CINCINNATI REGISTER
President Is To Speak To Women Of Nation, By Radio, October 7
The Depression from a Kid's Eye View
SATURDAY RADIO PROGRAM
BARGAIN WEEK-END FARES

KNITTED FOOTBALL FASHIONS

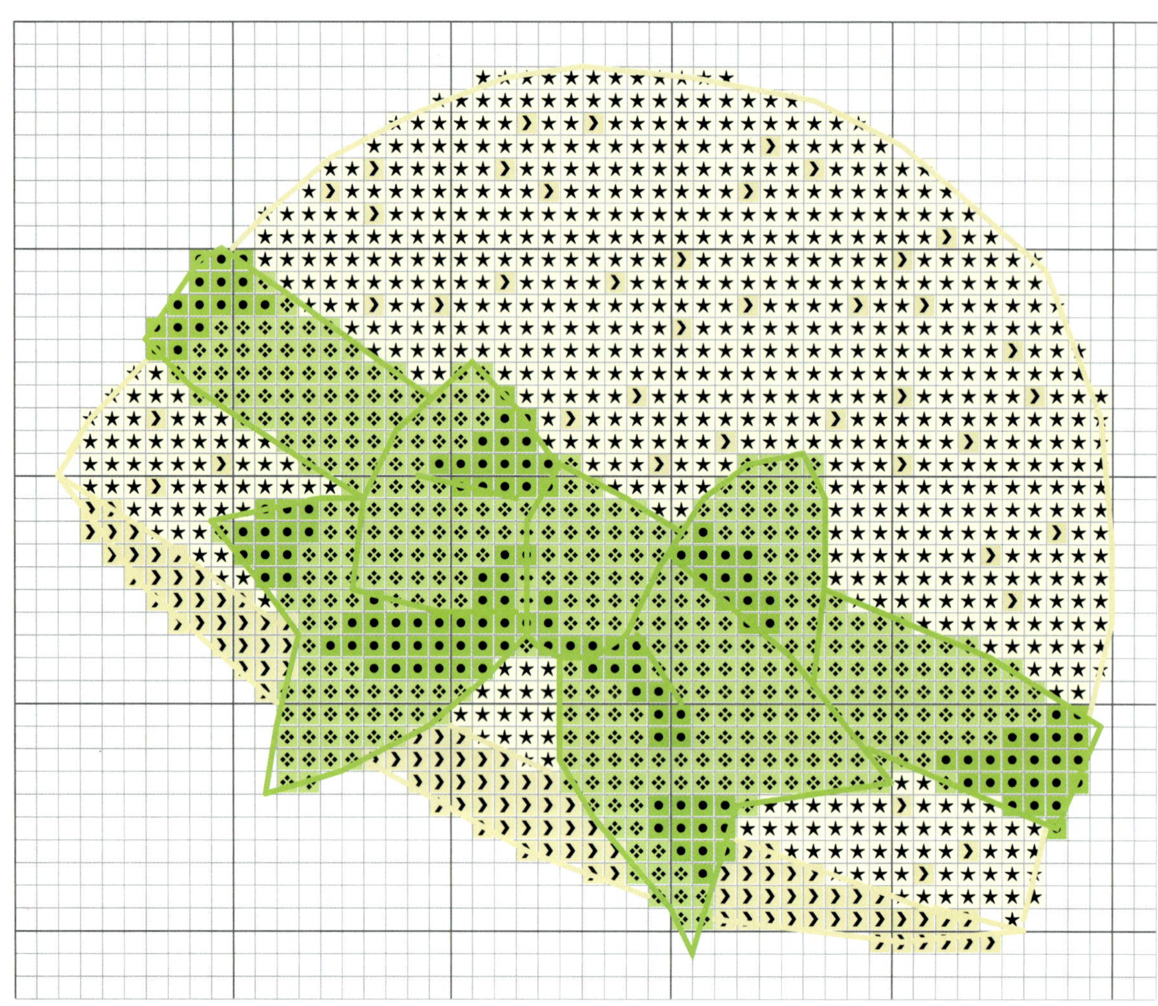

Legend:
- DMC-677
- DMC-704
- DMC-746
- DMC-3348

Backstitches:
- DMC-677
- DMC-704

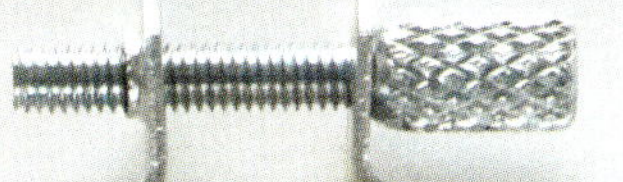

Julie

Times are a-changin', and Julie's not going to let anything keep her down. She's the optimist with a plan and stands up for what is right and equal, all the while brandishing a peace sign. When life throws everything into a state of flux, and who we are gets mired down by assumptions, we can look to Alley Oop herself for a bold, bright, and positive assist.

DIFFICULTY: Intermediate

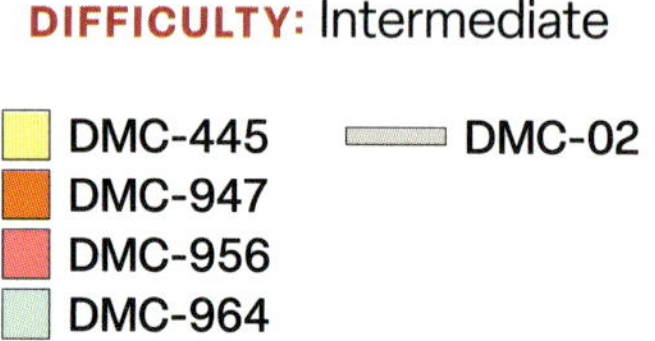

Finished size on 14-count Aida: 3.5" x 3"

Approximate stitch time: 6–7 hours

Aida fabric size: 8" x 8"

Display hoop size: 6–7" hoop

DOLL DEETS

In 1974, Julie Albright faces many challenges—her parents' divorce, moving to a new home, and fighting for a spot on the boys' basketball team. Through it all, she focuses on things that bring her joy, like her best friend Ivy Ling, another favorite American Girl; her love for books; and the totally groovy décor in her room.

LO
VE

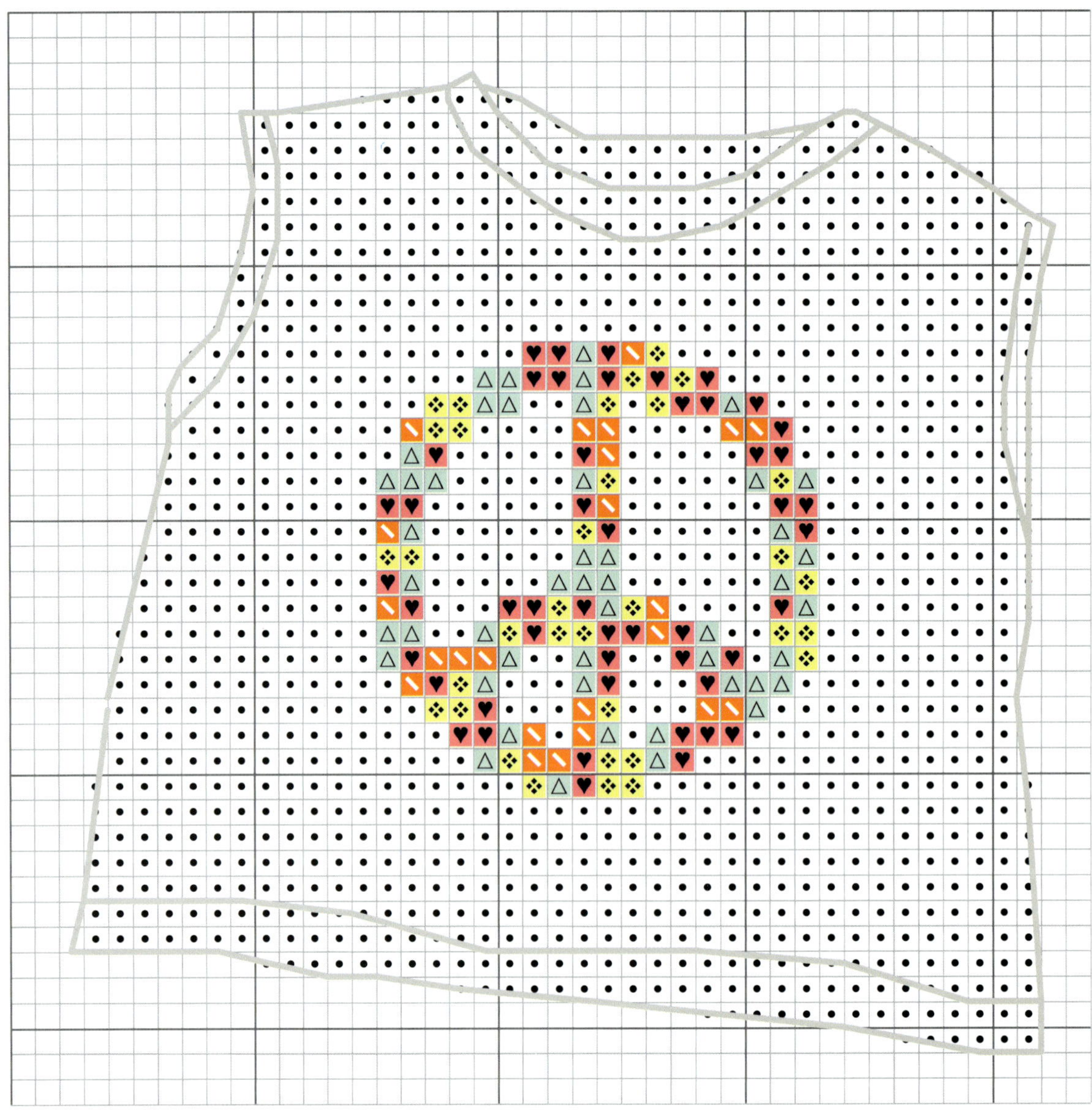

Legend:

- DMC-445
- DMC-947
- DMC-956
- DMC-964
- DMC-White

Backstitches:

- DMC-02

Josefina

Josefina longs for life to be the way it was when her Mamá was alive. She takes comfort in remembering the prayers and songs Mamá taught her. She wants to heal her family and help her sisters be at peace with one another. It's a tall order for such small shoulders, but our Josefina just wraps her shawl around her and keeps hoping and healing.

DIFFICULTY: Advanced

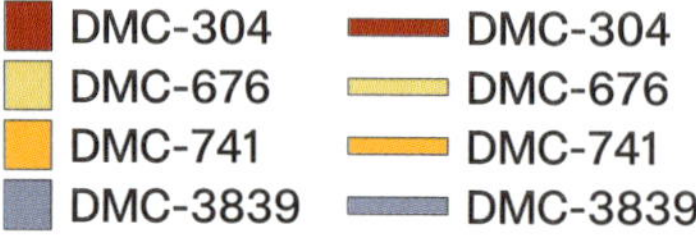

Finished size on 14-count Aida: 4.5" x 3.5"

Approximate stitch time: 7–8 hours

Aida fabric size: 8" x 8"

Display hoop size: 6–7" hoop

DOLL DEETS

Josefina Montoya's year is 1824. She lives on a rancho in New Mexico and dreams of being a healer like her godmother and aunt, Tía Magdalena. Her favorite flower is the primrose, and her least favorite goat is Florecita—especially after she eats Mamá's flower garden!

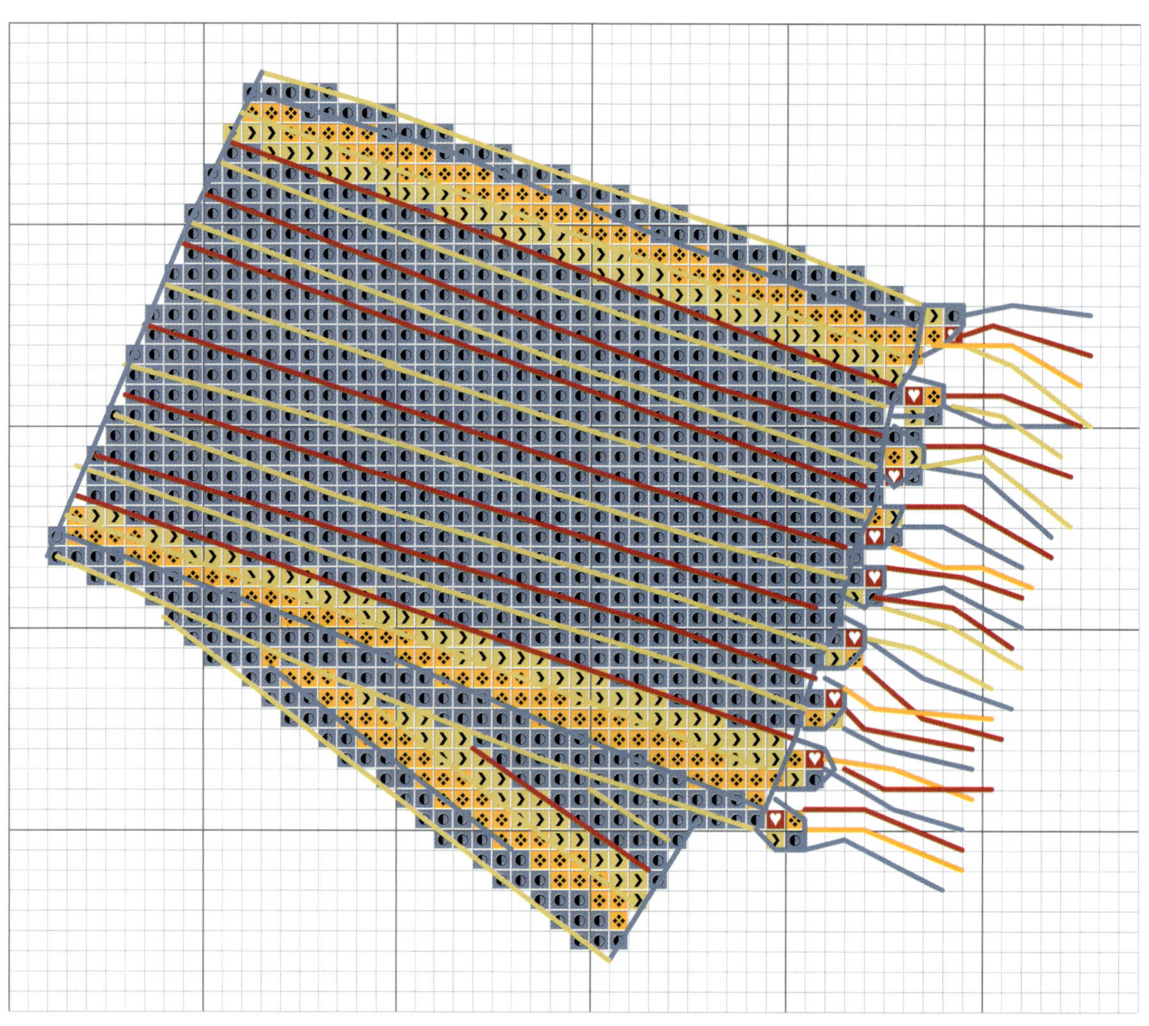

Legend:	Backstitches:
DMC-304	DMC-304
DMC-676	DMC-676
DMC-741	DMC-741
DMC-3839	DMC-3839

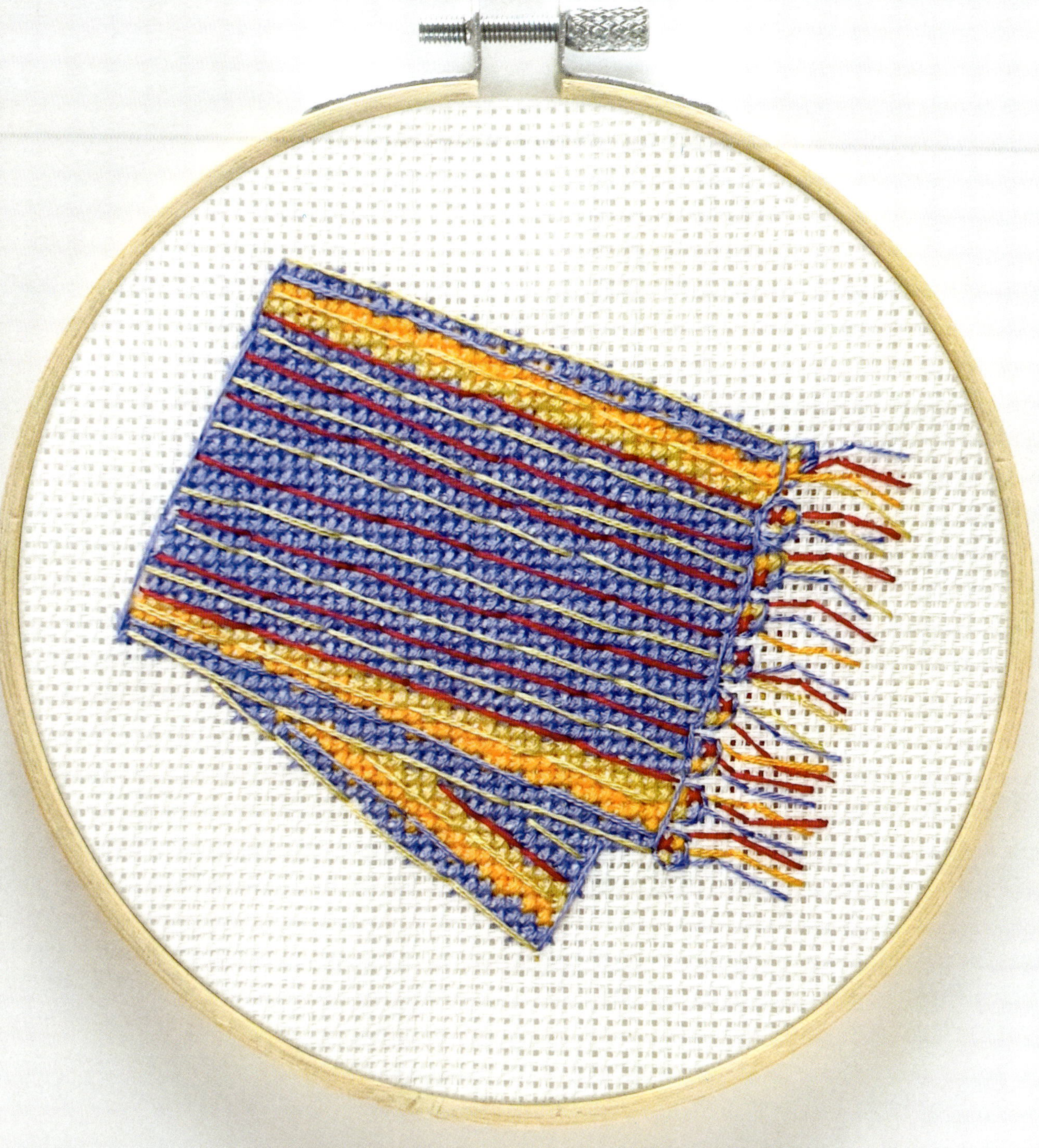

AmericanGirl
AmericanGirl
AmericanGirl
Summer MIX
Taffy

Part Three: AG Life

There are things that unite fans who grew up with American Girl—remembering the first time they picked up *The Care & Keeping of You*, reading the inspirational stories of the courageous characters, or trying their different hairstyles. No matter if you're a newcomer to the AG life or have been a fan for a while—there will always be a seat for you (and at the café, of course)!

TIP: If you're looking for ways to break free of the phone and forge deeper friendships, create a cross-stitch circle! Invite your American Girl(friends) to join you in stitching together. Meet up once a week at your favorite park or coffee shop to stitch and chat all things AG. Or if you live near a store, meet up there! It's the perfect place to sip and stitch.

Besties

Coconut and Licorice—the famously adorable duo of American Girl petdom. Bright-eyed and furry Licorice the cat loves to play with her Westie bestie, Coconut the dog. Stitch this for your bestie, or as an homage to the institution of friendship itself.

DIFFICULTY: Intermediate

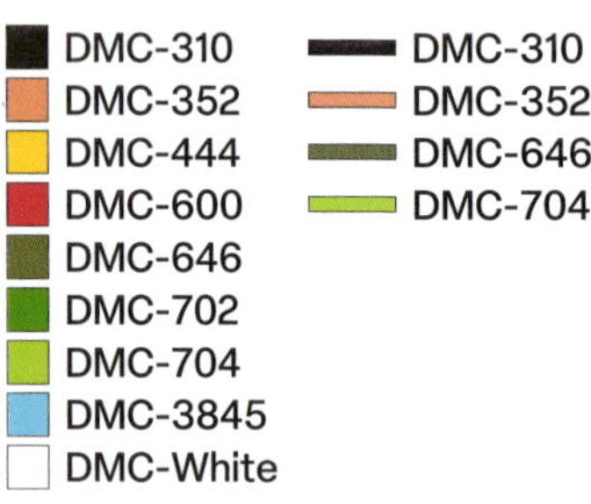

Finished size on 14-count Aida: 5" x 5"

Approximate stitch time: 7–8 hours

Aida fabric size: 9" x 9"

Display hoop size: 7–8" hoop

FUN FACTS

Licorice was formally known as Licorice Twist, and Coconut is called Coconut Chip. Because upping the cuteness factor is so American Girl!

Licorice

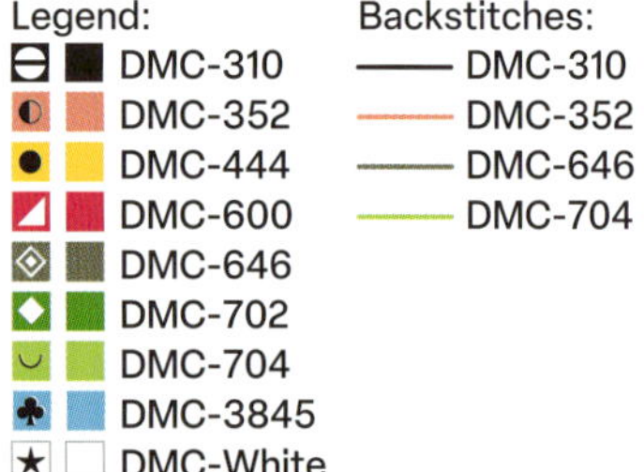
Legend:
DMC-310
DMC-352
DMC-444
DMC-600
DMC-646
DMC-702
DMC-704
DMC-3845
DMC-White
Backstitches:
DMC-310
DMC-352
DMC-646
DMC-704

Besties

The Care & Keeping of You

American Girl fans are unquestionably familiar with *The Care & Keeping of You*, the ever-popular guide to girlhood and growing up. Fans bask in the nostalgia tied to this seemingly timeless book, where everything we knew, we knew because of *The Care & Keeping of You*.

DIFFICULTY: Easy

- DMC-600 (full stitch)
- DMC-702 (full stitch)
- DMC-702 (backstitch)

Finished size on 14-count Aida: 5" x 5"
Approximate stitch time: 5–6 hours
Aida fabric size: 9" x 9"
Display hoop size: 7–8" hoop

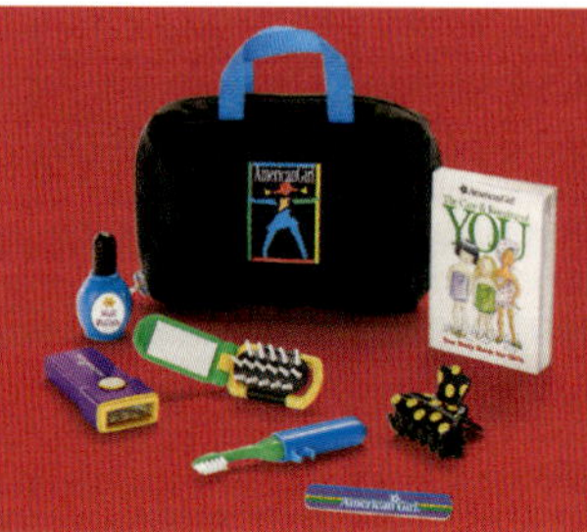

FUN FACTS

The Care & Keeping of You, launched in 1998, recently had its twenty-fifth anniversary. It's been a *New York Times* best seller numerous times and praised for its relevance and overall positive impact on millennial women, who were the book's target audience upon release.

American Girl
The Care & Keeping of
YOU

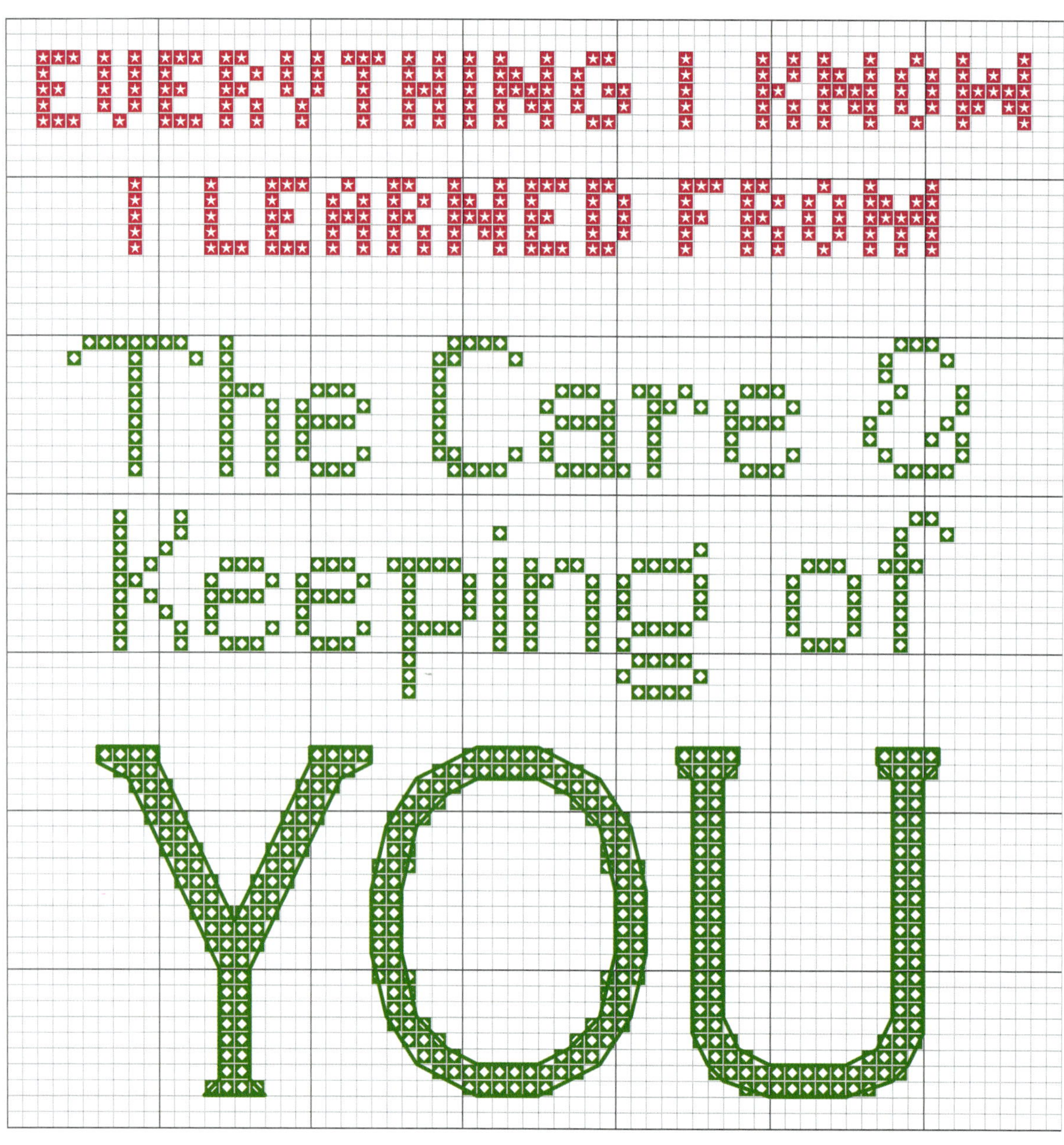

Legend:
DMC-600
DMC-702

Backstitches:
DMC-702

EVERYTHING I KNOW
I LEARNED FROM
The Care &
Keeping of
YOU

Style Icon

Molly's bag, Maryellen's necklace, Kirsten's bow, Josefina's earrings, and, of course, the classic American Girl hairbrush. These are some of the many style icons that true AG fans adore. Stitch this design in one glorious statement piece or stitch your favorite motifs individually.

DIFFICULTY: Advanced

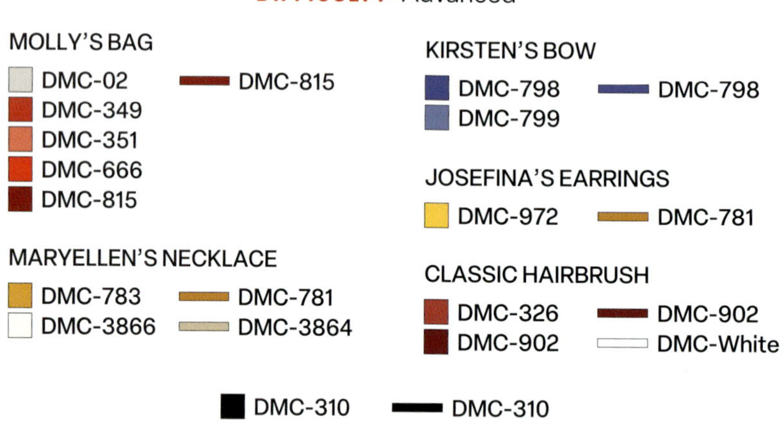

Finished size on 14-count Aida: 7.5" x 7.5"

Approximate stitch time: 10–12 hours

Aida fabric size: 11.5" x 11.5"

Display hoop size: 9–10" hoop

FUN FACTS

From the days of the original Pleasant Company, American Girl has focused on accuracy of style in clothing and accessories for all its Historical Characters. Pleasant Rowland made certain every detail of a character's dress and accessories accurately represented her time period. To this day, that commitment to accuracy is what modern fans have come to expect from American Girl.

Legend:
DMC-02
DMC-310
DMC-326
DMC-349
DMC-351
DMC-666
DMC-783
DMC-798
DMC-799
DMC-815
DMC-902
DMC-972
DMC-3866
Backstitches:
DMC-310
DMC-781
DMC-798
DMC-815
DMC-902
DMC-3864
DMC-White
Style
Icon

Style
Icon

Meet Me at the Café

The American Girl Café is more than just a pretty place with excellent cinnamon buns. It's a treasured space for fans, new and old. A place to gather, connect, reconnect, and reminisce. "Meet Me at the Café" is a call to girlhood's most cherished destination—a place to feel truly you.

DIFFICULTY: Intermediate

Finished size on 14-count Aida: 8" x 8"

Approximate stitch time: 10–12 hours

Aida fabric size: 12" x 12"

Display hoop size: 9–10" hoop

FUN FACTS

The American Girl Café has become a cult favorite among OG fans and a cherished meetup location. Fine dining with your favorite doll pals (not to mention your favorite dolls) is a thing. And in case you're not convinced, freshly baked cinnamon buns are the *starter*.

American Girl®
FUN AND GAMES

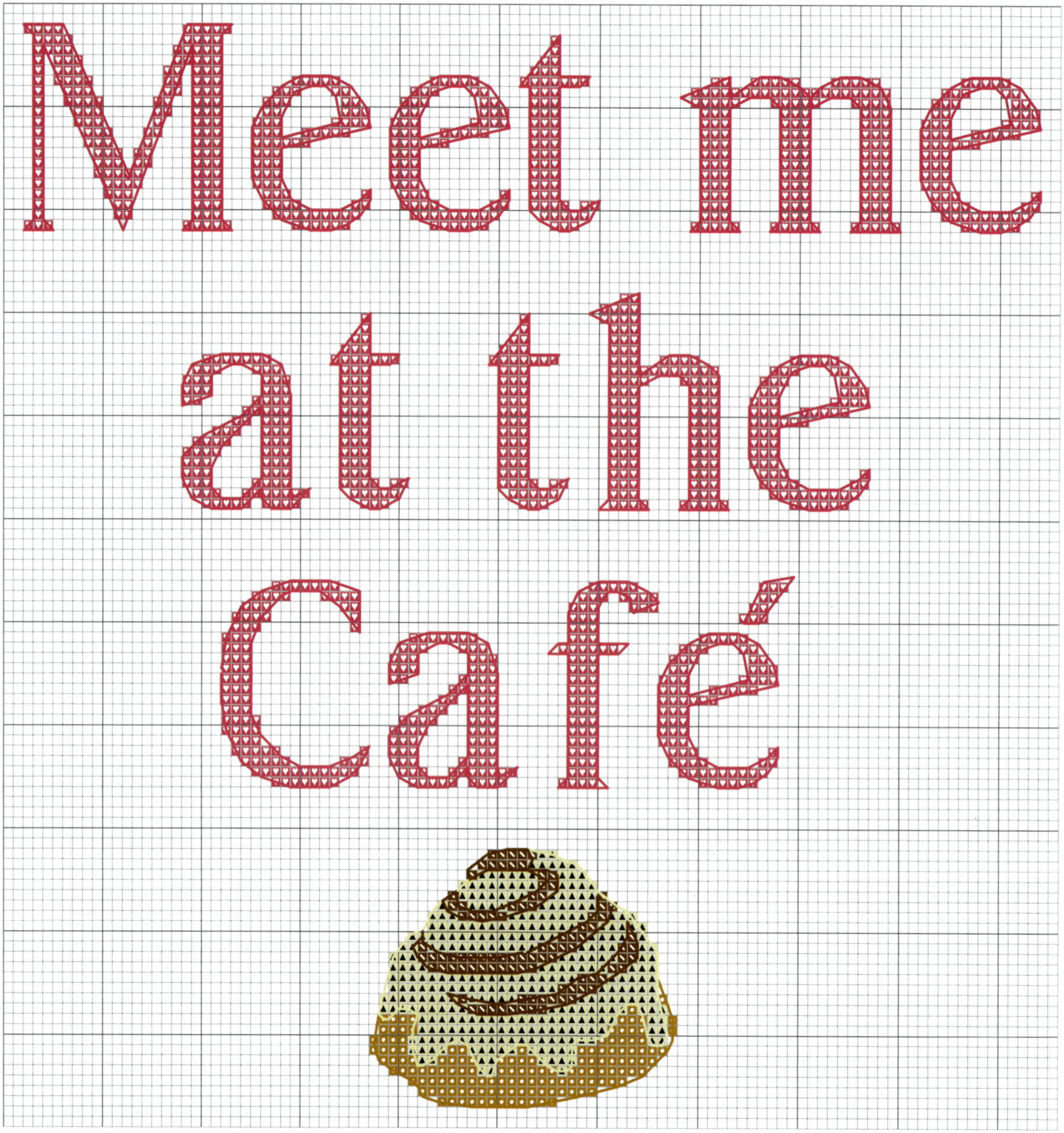

Meet me at the Café

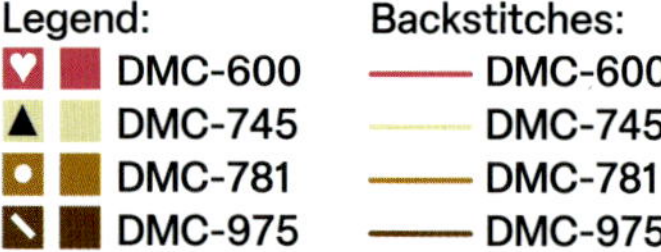

Legend:
- DMC-600
- DMC-745
- DMC-781
- DMC-975

Backstitches:
- DMC-600
- DMC-745
- DMC-781
- DMC-975

Meet me
at the
Café

Wear It Up

To wear your hair up or short means to have that extra bit of confidence and maturity. Perhaps even a sense of accomplishment—there are places to be, people to meet, things to do! Embrace your inner Kirsten, Addy, or Kit with these hairstyle silhouettes. The best part is you can stitch these designs individually.

DIFFICULTY: Intermediate

DMC-310	DMC-02
DMC-517	DMC-310
DMC-676	DMC-517
DMC-704	DMC-676
DMC-977	DMC-704
DMC-3846	DMC-977
DMC-White	DMC-3846

Finished size on 14-count Aida: 9" x 3"

Approximate stitch time: 8–10 hours

Aida fabric size: 13" x 13"

Display hoop size: 10–12" hoop

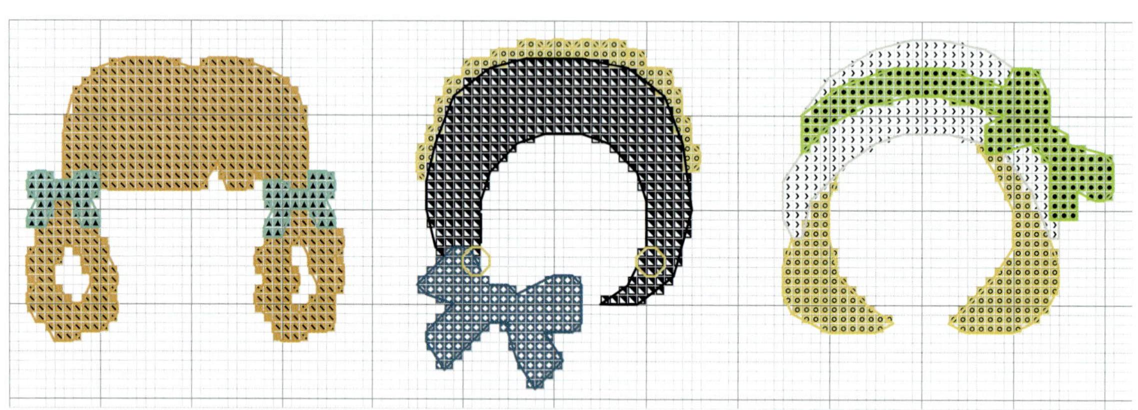

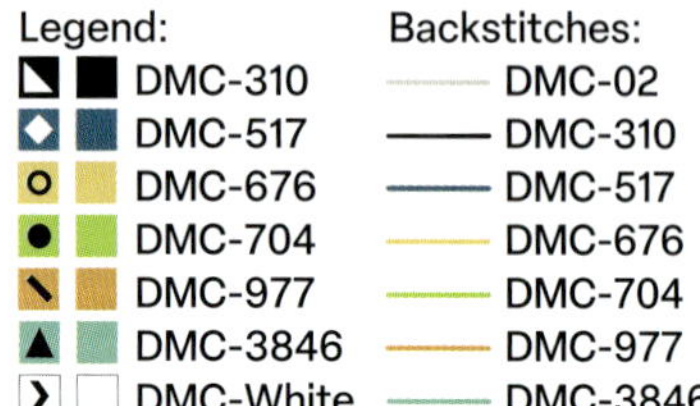
Legend:
DMC-310
DMC-517
DMC-676
DMC-704
DMC-977
DMC-3846
DMC-White
Backstitches:
DMC-02
DMC-310
DMC-517
DMC-676
DMC-704
DMC-977
DMC-3846

Dreaming of the Stars

American Girl raised a generation of girls to aspire to bigger and better things, to hope for what's sometimes beyond hope, and to allow time for dreaming. Best of all, the beloved characters of Molly, Kirsten, Addy, and the rest taught us how to act as much as to dream.

DIFFICULTY: Easy

Finished size on 14-count Aida: 8.5" x 7.5"

Approximate stitch time: 10–12 hours

Aida fabric size: 12.5" x 12.5"

Display hoop size: 10–12" hoop

TIP: Get cozy! No matter what time of year it is, needlework and a cozy drink (hot or iced) go well together. In fact, it's kind of a cross-stitch tradition.

Spelling Match
freedom
Carriage
Prince
family
AM

Dreaming
of
the
STARS

Legend:

- DMC-310
- DMC-444
- DMC-600
- DMC-702
- DMC-3845

Backstitches:

- DMC-310
- DMC-444
- DMC-600
- DMC-3845

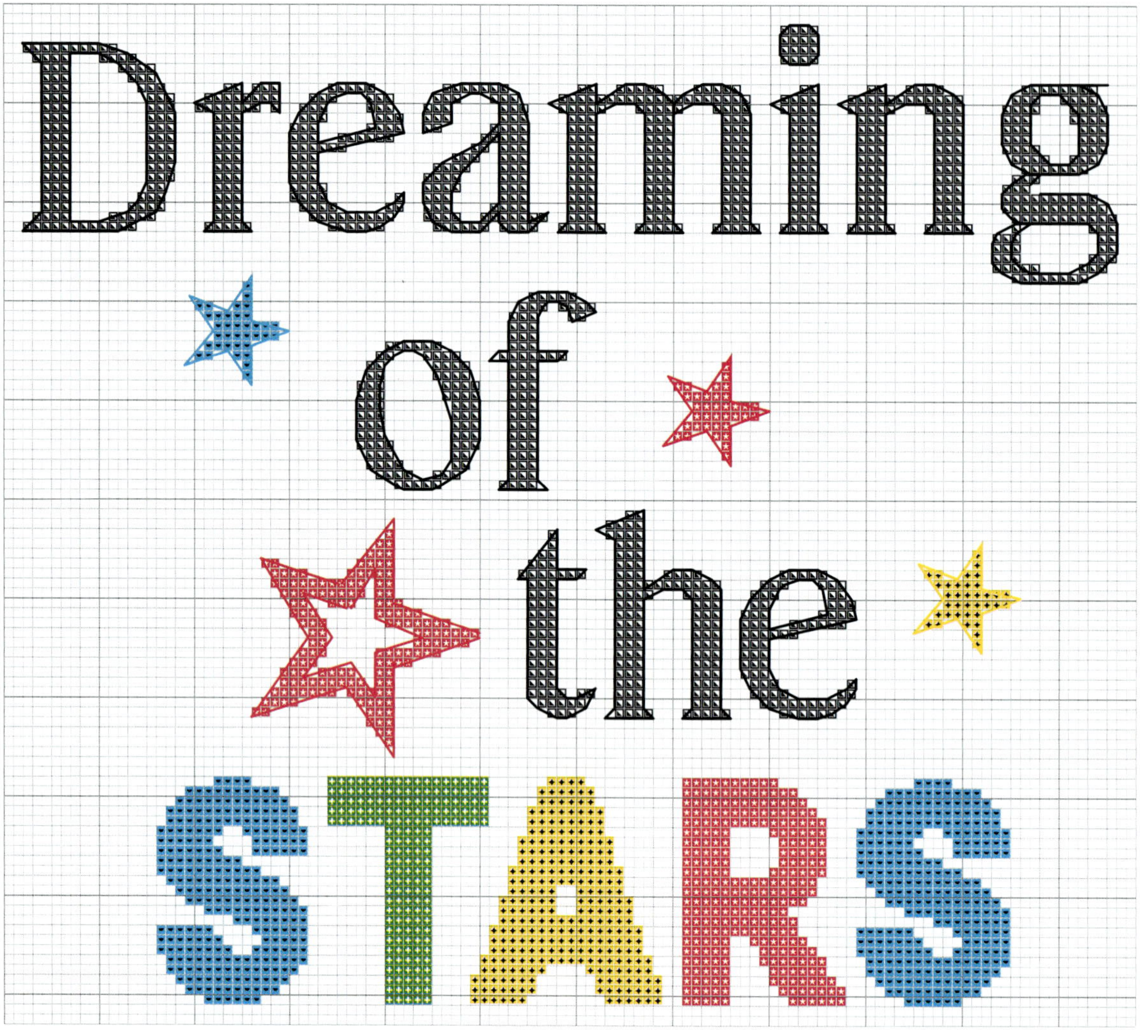

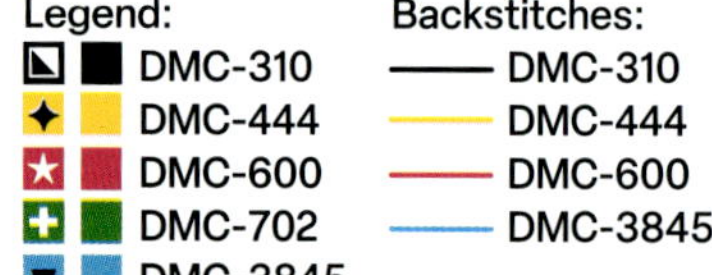

Dreaming
of
the
STARS

Wear It Down

To wear it down means there's a touch of the wild in you. A bit of the fierce. A little adventurousness perhaps. Embrace your inner Molly, Samantha, or Kaya. And just like the "Wear It Up" counterpart, you can single out your favorite hair silhouette and stitch it on its own.

DIFFICULTY: Intermediate

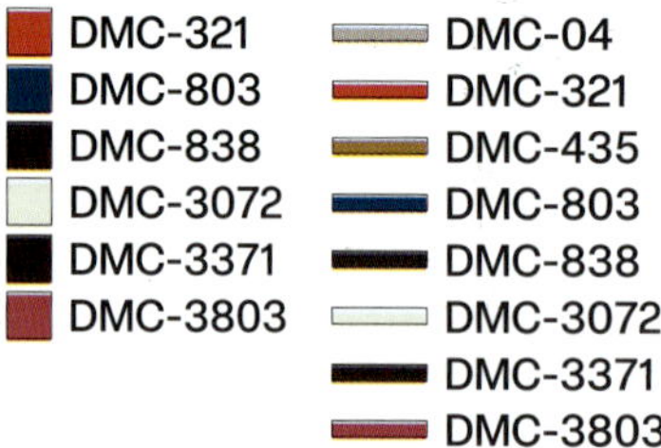

Finished size on 14-count Aida: 9" x 5.5"

Approximate stitch time: 8–10 hours

Aida fabric size: 13" x 13"

Display hoop size: 10–12" hoop

Molly

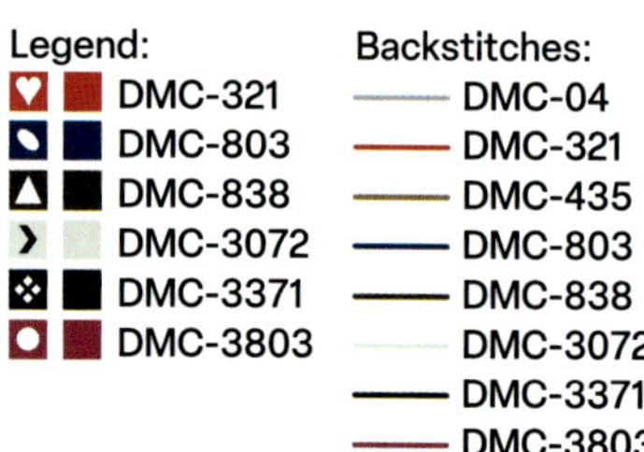

Legend:

- DMC-321
- DMC-803
- DMC-838
- DMC-3072
- DMC-3371
- DMC-3803

Backstitches:

- DMC-04
- DMC-321
- DMC-435
- DMC-803
- DMC-838
- DMC-3072
- DMC-3371
- DMC-3803

Raised by American Girl

If you were lucky enough to be raised by American Girl, then no explanation is necessary. Just that warm and cozy feeling of growing up reading about Kirsten, Addy, Samantha, and Molly, thumbing the pages of the beloved catalog, all while snuggling with your favorite doll. Life was good.

DIFFICULTY: Easy

DMC-310 DMC-310
DMC-600 DMC-600

Finished size on 14-count Aida: 8.5" x 5.5"
Approximate stitch time: 10–12 hours
Aida fabric size: 12.5" x 12.5"
Display hoop size: 10–12" hoop

Legend:

★ ■ DMC-310

♥ ■ DMC-600

Backstitches:

—— DMC-310

—— DMC-600

raised by
American
Girl

Walk Like an American Girl

Longtime fans well remember the classic book covers featuring Samantha, Kirsten, and Addy walking in their unique, now iconic strut. The American Girl walk is all about confidence and fortitude—meeting fate with a ribbon, a smile, and a heart of gold.

DIFFICULTY: Easy

Finished size on 14-count Aida: 6.5" x 4"

Approximate stitch time: 8–10 hours

Aida fabric size: 10.5" x 10.5"

Display hoop size: 8–10" hoop

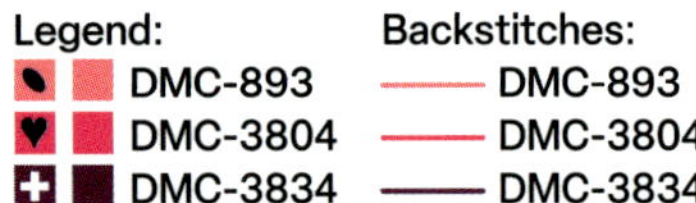
Legend:
DMC-893
DMC-3804
DMC-3834
Backstitches:
DMC-893
DMC-3804
DMC-3834

Rebel with a Hair Ribbon

The hair ribbon, like girlhood itself, is often overlooked as too sweet to be important and too frivolous to be of value. American Girl taught us that the opposite is true. A lot has been accomplished by people wearing hair ribbons. The best part is you don't need to doff the ribbon to be a rebel. Wear it with pride because it's hard to win a battle with your hair in your eyes.

DIFFICULTY: Intermediate

■ DMC-310 ▬ DMC-310
■ DMC-600 ▬ DMC-600

Finished size on 14-count Aida: 5" x 8"

Approximate stitch time: 12–14 hours

Aida fabric size: 12" x 12"

Display hoop size: 10–12" hoop

Legend:

DMC-310

DMC-600

Backstitches:

DMC-310

DMC-600

REBEL
WITH A
HAIR
RIBBON

Acknowledgments

This book has been a singularly wonderful experience to design and write. American Girl history and folklore are richer and deeper than we ever imagined. Tumbling down the rabbit hole we found ourselves in a world filled with wonder—the storybooks, the dolls, the details—every bit of which these newly minted adult fans find enchanting.

For this amazing experience, we'd like to warmly thank our editor, Maria Riillo. From the beginning, her enthusiasm and love for American Girl were thoroughly contagious. And as with all great editors, she guided and encouraged with a gentle hand. Thanks, Maria. So much.

Our deepest appreciation to everyone at Running Press who's had a hand in turning our manuscript into a beautiful, can't-believe-it's-true, honest-to-goodness book. So many talents, so much hard work—thank you all.

And of course, thanks to Mattel for taking up the torch from Pleasant Company and making American Girl the bold, bright, and beautiful thing that it is today. Fans young and old can cherish these characters and their stories and find a place that's safe, cozy, inspiring, and brimful of nostalgic goodness.

About the Authors

Sosae and Dennis Caetano are a wife and husband design team based in California, specializing in all things cute. For more than eight years, they've been designing for Trellis & Thyme, their popular needlecraft and quilt pattern company. Their kawaii cross-stitch designs appear regularly in the UK's *World of Cross Stitching* magazine, and they have over one hundred published cross-stitch and felt-embroidery patterns in *Cross Stitch Crazy* and *Mollie Makes* magazines. They are the authors of *Kawaii Craft Life* (Running Press, 2019), the *Kawaii Cross-Stitch Kit* (Running Press Minis, 2019), *Cute Kawaii Cross Stitch* (David & Charles, 2023), and *Gudetama Cross-Stitch* (Running Press, 2024).